ALSO BY GEORGE A. GLASS

COLD WAR DIPLOMAT
Inside U.S. Diplomacy
1981–2011

.

THE HAMILTONS

OF DANBURY

THE HAMILTONS OF DANBURY

1688–2015

Whales, Revolution, Wild West, Civil War, Printing Press

by

GEORGE A. GLASS

Printed in the United States of America

CWD
www.coldwardiplomat.com

ISBN 978-0-9863463-2-3

(CLOTH BOUND)

10 9 8 7 6 5 4 3 2 1

1. U.S. History 2. Civil War 3. Genealogy 4. Connecticut

First Edition

Dedicated to George Edgar Hamilton

A Grandfather with a Sense of History

CONTENTS

GENEALOGICAL NOTE

This work generally tracks the following genealogical lineage, including references to spouses and siblings, when such information was available and relevant.

GALLATIN HAMILTON	1622–1720
WILLIAM HAMILTON	1643–1746
JOSEPH HAMILTON	1693–1778
SILAS HAMILTON	1726–1790
JOHN HAMILTON	1754–1803
ELI HAMILTON	1783–1867
NORMAN B. HAMILTON	1807–1873
GEORGE NORRIS HAMILTON	1830–1901
EDGAR EDWARD HAMILTON	1860–1919
GEORGE EDGAR HAMILTON	1892–1964
GEORGE NEWTON HAMILTON	1925–1999

PREFACE

At some point the ghost of curiosity seems to compel one to venture into the attic, to either condemn memories to the dust bin, or to wade into those memories, thick as a spooky forest on a moonless night. Such ventures entail risk, reaching into the suffocating dust of centuries past to extract what may be at best a piecemeal recounting, usually stimulating more questions than answers, but inevitably firing doubts about one's prior points of reference.

My attic was rather difficult to locate. It began with a phone call in early January 2009 from a gentleman introducing himself to me as my brother. Up until that time I had not been aware of having any siblings, having been raised an only child in southern New Jersey. But it appears that my biological father had generated two additional offspring with the woman for whom he deserted my mother and I. Over the ensuing months, I came to get to know a bit of my new half-brother. After a few months he mailed me an envelope containing numerous documents, letters and photos from the world of my biological father, whom I had not known since the age of two.

Among those treasures was the original written will of my grandfather, George Edgar Hamilton. In Item III of that will, written on August 17, 1959, Hamilton bequeathed to the Connecticut State Library in Hartford, Connecticut, his collection of Hamilton family papers, consisting of wills, deeds, letters, diaries, etc., from the time of the Revolution to the end of the 19th century. This was my attic.

In subsequent years I have spent hours in that library ruminating over the crumbling, oft-indecipherable scribling's and scraps of centuries past. Why did anyone think these documents were worthy of retention or review? It was not clear at all what linked these documents. Grade school report cards from 1873. An antique photo without a name. Dozens of pre-revolutionary land deeds bearing the seal of the English king. A diary of a trip out West. Letters home. Why were they kept? Why were they important? Why, indeed, should a library retain such a collection under the very tightest of security to protect the integrity of the crumbling paper? It was a multi-year struggle to find my way through a substantial portion of these holdings.

The following recounting is an effort to recreate and bring to light, in a semi-readable form, some of the more enigmatic anecdotes woven amidst these relics from the attic. The stories emerge from the trials and tragedies of the Hamilton Family of Danbury, a family that settled there before the Revolution, and did not leave until the late 20th century. In the end, I have become convinced that this family retained these records, in their disorganized and oft-illegible form, because family members knew that they were part of something at the time. Whether it was a sense of the founding period of a struggling country, the perilous nature of the wars they confronted, the pursuit of Manifest Destiny, the advent of modernity and the printing press, a reaction against the onslaught of history, or an act of self-reflection, their attic has made for a lively romp for me for several years.

The specific recountings of challenges in the Minnesota Territory of 1856, and the profound commitment of the family to fighting, and describing, key battles of the Civil War, provide a flavorful sense of those times. Given the relative abundance of materials, these events became the somewhat larger focus of this work. Nonetheless, the rather curious and unique experiences afflicting the Hamiltons since they first landed in the New World three centuries ago, provide a colorful reminder of the hardships and extreme uncertainties of times past.

I have endeavored to present as cogently as possible at this time their stories, which are a microcosm of the history unfolding around them through the centuries. Where possible, I have been able to provide a number of photos of some of the central players, images recovered from the far recesses of another distant, and previously unknown, relative's collection. I have then tried to weave the original documents and photos into a modest retelling, substantiated by a number of historical books and references, of this one family in

Danbury. I have tried to preserve the original language of transcribed documents to the extent possible, while distilling some sense of the meaning. Such accountings invariably create more questions than answers, and underscore the absence of many facts. Yet, I suspect that as of this writing, no other person has examined this repository of history since its commitment to the basement of the Connecticut State Library in 1964.

Above all else, this endeavor gave me pause to reconsider the specific details of living in America, as it was born, as it was tried, and as it has endured.

George A. Glass
December 2015
Garmisch-Partenkirchen

CHAPTER ONE

OF WHALES & WITCHCRAFT
(1668)

*T*here are numerous and somewhat varying accounts of the Hamilton family of Danbury. Though not among the original eight founding families of the town, the family nonetheless does feature on and off through the generations as having been active in the sometimes colorful history and life of the town up to the 21st century. Though there appear to have been more than one such-named family in Danbury, all of the Hamiltons in this writing derive from one Scottish origin, Gallatin Hamilton, a physician from Glasgow. There are differences in the recounting of that origin, which seems to reflect that anecdotes were passed along verbally, and certain details were conveyed in different words over time. Nonetheless, the variations add to the mystique and, sometimes, mercurial nature of the family's origin. The main thrust of the story of origin is somewhat constant along the following lines from James Bailey's unique 1896 book on the *History of Danbury*:

The first ancestor of the Hamilton family in this country was William, a son of Gallatin Hamilton, of Glasgow,

Scotland. William was born in Glasgow in 1643; came early to New England; settled in Cape Cod, and was persecuted as one who dealt with evil spirits, for having killed the first whale on the New England Coast. He afterward went to South Kingston, R.I., and then came to Danbury, where he died in 1746, aged 103 years. This is a matter of family record, and also of antiquarian history. [1]

WHALE FISHERY, CURRIER & IVES
(SOURCE: US LIBRARY OF CONGRESS)

Bailey does not offer any source material for his recounting. He was a newpaper person, though, who collected stories and anecdotes from the town over many years.

A slightly different, second version of this story, from Robert E. Jenkins in 1904, adds that Gallatin Hamilton was

1   James Montgomery Bailey, *History of Danbury, Conn. 1684–1896* (New York: Burr Printing House, 1896), p. 67.

a physician in Glasgow, and that the son, William, was born in March 1647. It also names William's wife. Accordingly, William Hamilton:

> *Came to America, settled first on Cape Cod, Mass, re-*
> *moved to North Kingston, R.I., in 1668, died in Dan-*
> *bury, Conn., in 1749, aged one hundred and two years.*
> *Married Lucy, Mercy or Mary Berry, who was from En-*
> *gland. It is said that he was the first person who killed*
> *a whale along Cape Cod coast. The achievement was*
> *deemed so marvelous that his neighbors thought he*
> *must be in league with evil spirits. For this reason they*
> *persecuted him, and he changed his residence to Rhode*
> *Island.* [2]

This recounting is also reflected in substance in the 1851 work of early historian Samuel Drake. [3]

Such a story of whaling and witchcraft surely contributed to a certain magical aura around the first immigrant Hamilton. It was the kind of anecdote people were unlikely to forget. Hence the early Hamilton endured in history books. Indeed, a third version of events, dated from 1851, is the earliest printed recounting. It added some more speculation about whaling:

---

2   Robert E. Jenkins, *Jenkins Family Book Being a Partial Record of the Descendants of David Jenkins* (Chicago: Chicago Bar, 1904), p. 156.

3   Samuel G. Drake, editor, *New England Historical & Genealogical Register for the year 1851, Vol. V* (Boston: Samuel G. Drake, 1851), p. 456.

It is said that the first person who killed a whale upon this coast was a Scotchman, named William Hamilton, who "in early life settled on Cape Cod, whence he removed to Rhode Island, he being persecuted for killing the whale, by the inhabitants of the Cape, as one who dealt with evil spirits." Hamilton died in Connecticut in 1746, aged 103 years. This must have occurred some time prior to 1690, when the art of taking whales with boats from the shore was introduced at Nantucket by Ichabod Paddock from Cape Cod. [4]

Additional details about Hamilton, whaling and witch-craft are few. There are reports that William arrived at Cape Cod in 1668. [5] One early report from 1676, however, notes that a "William Hamelton (*sic*), a merchant" sought in February 1675 to hire a small vessel of 20 tons, for which he then paid 12 li. 10 s. per month in current silver of New England. [6] Others say that Hamilton moved in 1727 to New London, Connecticut before moving to Danbury, Connecticut, in 1738. Some note that when William and Mercy moved to Danbury, they were of an "advanced age."

4   Samuel Greene Arnold, *History of the State of Rhode Island and Providence Plantations Vol. II. 1701–1790* (Providence, R.I.: Preston & Rounds, 1894), p. 103.

5   David Dobson, *Scots in New England 1623–1873* (Baltimore, Md.: Genealogical Publishing Co., Inc., 2002), p. 93.

6   *Records and Files of the Quarterly Courts of Essex County Massachusetts, Volume VI, 1675–1678* (Salem, Massachusetts: Essex Institute, 1917), p. 197.

There are numerous recountings that William and Mercy were married sometime between 1668 and 1687, with 1683 perhaps supported as the most likely date. This may be supported by the fact that their first child was reportedly born in 1685. Still, historian Gertrude Wickham recounted that William Hamilton:

> *met on the boat an English girl named Mercy Berry. Both were homesick and longed for friends. Their mutual friendship grew and upon arriving they were married.* [7]

According to author Wayne Hamilton, the **Biographical Review of Delaware County, N.Y.** (BRDC), states that William Hamilton came to reside on Bear Mountain, in the Pembroke area of Danbury. He notes that William Hamilton:

> *Came to America and settled in Massachusetts in 1668. Later he removed to North Kingston, R.I. where he married Mercy Berry....After living in Rhode Island until their children were grown, Mr. and Mrs. Hamilton (advanced in years) removed to Danbury, Conn., (establishing his home on Bear mountain), where the former*

---

7   Gertrude Van Rensselaer Wickham and Mrs. Charles Heber Smith, *Memorial to the Pioneer Women of the Western Reserve* (Part 5) (Cleveland, OH: The Juson Company, 1924), p. 838.

died at the home of a son-in-law, Thomas Benedict, in May 1749, at the great age of 102 years. [8]

However, this passage does not seem to exist in the **Biographical Review** referenced by Wayne Hamilton, so it's sourcing is unclear. Nevertheless, references to William in the collection of Hamilton Family Records in the Connecticut State Library are numerous, including references to his "rocking chair" and cane, which were passed down as family heirlooms. [9]

Accounts of the numerous children deriving from William and Mercy also vary. The lists are long. William and Mercy may have had up to 10 children. One of the more fulsome descriptions from 1894 states that:

Their children were as follows: (1) Elizabeth, who married a Mr. Roberts, and died at the age of one hundred and two years; (2) Joseph, born in 1693, died in Redding, Conn., aged eighty-six years; (3) Thankful, married to a Mr. Sweet, and died aged one hundred and two years; (4) William. Jr., who settled in Rhode Island,

---

8   Wayne Hamilton, *The Hamilton Inheritance* (Snohomish County, Washington: Wayne Hamilton, 2001), pp. 3-4. Though Wayne Hamilton attributes this quoted passage to the *Biographical Review of Delaware County, N.Y.*, research for this current book has failed to confirm the precise passage in the *Review*.

9   Frank Lorenzo Hamilton in a letter to Edgar Eli Hamilton dated July 20, 1894. The original letter is in the **Hamilton–Knapp Collection 1742–1924** (Hartford: Connecticut State Library, Archive RG 69:7).

and died when ninety-eight years old; (5) David, born in North Kingston, Conn., April 11, 1697, died in Sharon, Conn., in 1779 at the age of eighty-two years; (6) Benjamin, born in 1701, a blacksmith for 70 years, died aged ninety-five; (7) Elisha, drowned at an early age; (8) Nathaniel, killed by a fall from a tree; (9) John, died young; [10]

Another historian notes that another child (10), Mary, was born in 1705, died with smallpox in 1757, was married to Thomas Benedict, and herself bore 11 children. [11]

All of the specific facts are not correct. Therefore a degree of guesstimating events is needed. Piecing different snippets of information together with information from the Hamilton family files suggests the following profiles for the 10 children, all of who were born in North Kingstown, Washington, Rhode Island: [12]

Elizabeth was born about 1685, married Mr. Roberts and died December 8, 1787, in East Haven, Connecticut. Her husband pre-deceased her.

Thankful was born about 1689, married William Sweet in 1708, and died about 1792 in Rhode Island. Her husband

---

10   *Commemorative Biographical Record of the Counties of Huron and Lorain, Ohio* (Chicago: J.H. Beers & Co., 1894), pp. 828–831.

11   Wayne Hamilton, *The Hamilton Inheritance* (Snohomish County, Washington: Wayne Hamilton, 2001) , pp 3–4.

12   *Hamilton–Knapp Collection 1742–1924* (Hartford: Connecticut State Library, Archive RG 69:7).

came originally from Warwickshire, England, where he was
born August 1, 1663. He died in Lake George, New York, on
November 10, 1728.

David was born March 31, 1697, and died about 1779
in Sharon, Connecticut. He married Anne Wright on August 23, 1727.

William Jr. was born about 1690, settled in Rhode Island, and died about 1788 in Danbury. He married Sarah
Benedict.

Elisha was born about 1700 and drowned at an early
age.

Benjamin was born about 1701, worked as blacksmith
for 70 years, and died about 1796.

John was born about 1702 and died young.

Mary was born about 1705, died from smallpox in
1757, and was married to Thomas Benedict, a Danbury official who notarized many of the later Hamilton land deeds
and was reportedly present at the death of William Hamilton. [13] Benedict was a descendant from one of Danbury's
eight founding families. Mary bore 11 children.

Nathaniel was born about 1707 and died from a fall
from a tree.

---

13   Wayne Hamilton, *The Hamilton Inheritance* (Snohomish
County, Washington: Wayne Hamilton, 2001), pp. 3–4.

Joseph was born about 1693. By one unsubstantiated account he married Susannah Eliza Castle, and died about 1778 in Redding, Connecticut. [14] However, official records for the Danbury probate district establish that Joseph died before April 7, 1778 (the actual date his estate was inventoried), in Danbury and that his widow was named Ruth. [15]

If all of the children were indeed born in Rhode Island, this suggests that William Hamilton did not move to Danbury until after 1707, when he was over 60 years of age. Joseph Hamilton, his eldest son, and Mary went with him. They settled on Bear Mountain.

Joseph and Ruth Hamilton lived in Danbury. Ruth's origins are unknown. She appears to have died in 1772 and he died intestate in 1778 in Danbury. They had five children, all delineated in probate records as follows:

(1) Ruth was the eldest daughter. She married John Cornwill of Danbury. She died around 1800 in Danbury.

(2) Silas was the eldest son. He was born in 1726, married Elizabeth Knapp, and died in November 1790.

---

14   Frank Lorenzo Hamilton in a letter to Edgar Eli Hamilton dated April 11, 1911. The original letter is in the *Hamilton–Knapp Collection 1742–1924* (Hartford: Connecticut State Library, Archive RG 69:7).

15   See Joseph Hamilton, Inventory of the Estate of Joseph Hamilton, 1778, and *Distribution of the Estate of Joseph Hamilton, 1778* (Danbury: Danbury Probate District #2162 (1778).

(3) William was the second eldest son. He married Sarah Benedict, a descendant of one of Danbury's eight founding families.

(4) Catherina was born in June 1730, married Nathaniel Gregory, and died April 13, 1810.

(5) Joseph, the youngest son, was born in 1732, married Thankful Taylor, and resided in Danbury. They in turn had four children, one of whom was named Joseph Hamilton Jr. [16] This appears to have been the same Joseph Hamilton Jr. who served during the Revolutionary War as drummer in Captain Noble Benedict's company, which was formed in 1775. According to Bailey, this was the only home-grown company Danbury provided during the Revolutionary War. Others in Danbury enlisted with units based out of other towns. [17] Joseph Hamilton Jr. was said to have resided in Pembroke, "which appears to have been a very patriotic portion of the town." [18]

Upon the death of the elder Joseph Hamilton (son of William), his widow Ruth and each of the five children received part of a multi-acre estate that included several houses. But it was Silas, the elder son, who became the entrepreneurial landholder in the family and an officer before and during the Revolution.

16   *Commemorative Biographical Record of Huron and Lorain, Ohio* (Chicago: J.H.Beers & Co., 1894), p. 831.

17   James Montgomery Bailey, *History of Danbury, Conn. 1684–1896* (New York: Burr Printing House, 1896), p. 56.

18   Ibid., p. 58.

CHAPTER TWO

REVOLUTIONARY WAR: THE RED CAPE ESCAPE

(1774–1777)

*I*n May 1754 the Connecticut Assembly established and confirmed Silas Hamilton to be lieutenant of the 2nd company or trainband in the town of Danbury, and ordered that he be commissioned accordingly.[1] In this year, the first skirmishes of the French and Indian Wars began in what is now western Pennsylvania. French authorities clashed with Virginia scouting parties led by George Washington. Even though Silas was commissioned in that year, the Connecticut Colony did not begin to mobilize until March 1755, when the General Assembly authorized bonuses and set salaries for military recruits. Hundreds of Connecticut militia marched to nearby Albany for the campaigns that followed. [2] The war officially ended in 1763. In May

---

1   Charles J. Hoadly, editor, *Public Records of the Colony of Connecticut, from May, 1754, to February, 1757, Inclusive* (Hartford: Press of the Case, Lockwood & Brainard Co., 1881), p. 264.

2   David Drury, "Connecticut in the French and Indian War," Undated, <http://www.connecticuthistory.org> (18 September 2015).

1762 the Connecticut Assembly promoted Silas Hamilton to captain of the 2nd company or trainband in Danbury in the 4th regiment in the colony. [3] During these years, the Connecticut Assembly remained loyal to England, though occasionally suffering from war-weariness and costs. The author has uncovered no evidence of actual participation by Silas Hamilton in any of the skirmishes or battles in the French and Indian Wars despite his commission.

However, several years later Silas Hamilton is mentioned in numerous books for narrowly evading death at the hands of the British during the notorious burning of Danbury in April 1777. In Bailey's authoritative account:

> *It was between two and three o'clock in the afternoon when the British arrived. The leader having selected his headquarters, the quartering of the force for the protection of themselves was next attended to. Tryon's assistants, Generals Erskine and Agnew, accompanied by a body of mounted infantry, proceeded up Main Street to the junction of the Barren Plain Road (now White Street), where Benjamin Knapp lived. His house stood where is now the Nichol's brick block, long known as Military Hall, the corner of which is now occupied as a drug store.*

---

3   Charles J. Hoadly, **Public Records of the Colony of Connecticut, from May, 1762, to October, 1767, Inclusive** (Hartford: Press of the Case, Lockwood & Brainard Co., 1881), p. 15.

The two generals quartered themselves upon Mr. Knapp, taking complete possession of the house, with the exception of one room, where Mrs. Knapp was lying ill.

On this dash up Main Street the party met with two incidents. Silas Hamilton had a piece of cloth at a fuller's on South Street. It is said that Major Taylor was the fuller. When Hamilton heard of the approach of the enemy, he mounted his horse and rode off at full speed for his goods. He was rather late, however, and when he came out to remount his horse, a squad of the force was upon him. He flew up Main Street with a half dozen troopers in full pursuit, and on reaching West Street he turned into it, with the hair on his head very erect.

The pursuers followed him, and one in advance and close upon him swung his sword to cut him down, when a singular but most fortunate accident occurred. Hamilton lost a part of his hold on the roll, to which he had until this time tenaciously clung, and the cloth flew out like a giant ribbon, frightening the pursing animals and rendering them unmanageable, so Mr. Hamilton escaped with his cloth.

The column that came up Main Street were fired upon from the house of Captain Ezra Starr, which stood where now is the residence of Mrs. D. P. Nichols, corner of Main and Boughton Streets. The shots, it has been claimed, were fired by four young men. It was an act of reckless daring and the actors must have been very young, as the shots could have had no other effect than to exasperate the invaders.

The men who fired on the enemy, from Captain Starr's house, were killed, and their bodies were burned in the building; but there were not four of them, there were three. One was a negro, named Adams. The two white men were Joshua Porter and Eleazer Starr. The former was a member of Noble Benedict's company, organized in 1775. He was great-grandfather of Colonel Samuel Gregory of this town, and lived in that part of the town that is called Westville District. He was in the village after a gallon of molasses when the enemy came. Starr lived where now stands the News building. [4]

In the night following these events, Colonial soldiers marched toward Danbury. As the British began to evacuate, they burned many of the homes and stores in the city. In the probate record of the will of Silas Hamilton in 1793 (as well as in land records), Silas is referred to as "Captain" Silas Hamilton, suggesting that he retained his military rank and commission through the Revolution.

Some uncertainty must be acknowledged by the author as to whether the Silas Hamilton fleeing the British as recounted here was the father, Captain Silas Hamilton, or rather his son, Silas Hamilton Jr. The **Biographical Record of Fairfield County Connecticut Part II** asserts that it was Silas

---

4 James Montgomery Bailey, *History of Danbury, Conn. 1684–1896* (New York: Burr Printing House, 1896), p. 66–67.

Hamilton Jr. [5] The *Biographical Record* was certainly written with input from descendant Edgar Edward Hamilton (see Chapter 9) at the time of its publication in 1899. However, there appear to be numerous facts in the *Biographical Record* that are at odds with other proven documents on the Hamiltons. The *History of Fairfield County*, on the other hand, suggests that the story is about Captain Silas Hamilton the elder; namely, the author refers to Hamilton as "old daddy" and "the old gentleman." [6] In any event, the Hamiltons now had another colorful and especially memorable story to add to the family history in the making.

Captain Silas Hamilton was a major landowner in the Bear Mountain area of the Danbury-Pembroke district. The Hamilton-Knapp Collection includes some 50 or more land records/deeds dating from 1742 onwards, most of which derive from dealings by Silas Hamilton. However, these deeds are difficult to delineate on a map since they marked land with references to such things as a large stone in the northwest corner of a field, or as far as a neighbors fence, or up to a stream or a large tree. Time has erased most of the markers. Hence it becomes almost impossible to ascertain the precise modern location of this expansive acreage.

---

5   *Commemorative Biographical Record of Fairfield County, Connecticut, Part II* (Chicago: J.H. Beers & Co., 1899) p. 918.

6   D. Hamilton Hurd, editor, *History of Fairfield County, Connecticut* (Philadelphia: J.W. Lewis & Co., 1881) p. 642.

Silas and Elizabeth had six children as follows, all of whom were born in Danbury: [7]

Elizabeth, who married Lemeul Lindsley on May 27, 1773.

James, who died in 1779.

Orpha, who married Abijah Barnum on October 20, 1763.

Silas Jr., who was born in 1745 and died in 1825. He married Hannah Hoyt on July 22, 1763.

Paul, who was born November 19, 1752, married Anna Stevens, sister of Anner Stevens, both of whom were daughters of Lieutenant Ezra Stevens of Danbury. Paul died May 31, 1830. He was a captain in the Colonial Army.

John, who was born in 1754, married Anner Stevens (sister of Anna Stevens) of Danbury, and was found frozen to death on January 12, 1803.

John and Anner lived in Danbury. Anner was the daughter of renowned Lieutenant Ezra Stevens, who was in the Revolutionary War. Ezra Stevens was born May 25, 1724, in Danbury and died February 6, 1825. He is buried in the Old North Burying Grounds (also called North Main Street Cemetery) in Danbury. He was commissioned 2nd

---

[7]   Children's names from the *1785 Will of Silas Hamilton*, Probated in Danbury, Connecticut on November 13, 1790.

lieutenant on May 1, 1775, in Captain Noble Benedict's 6th Company of Colonel David Waterbury's 5th Continental Regiment. The regiment was recruited mainly in Fairfield County and first marched to New York under General David Wooster and then to the Northern Department. The term of service expired in December 1775, but due to illness, many men returned home in October and November. Ezra Stevens was discharged on October 29, 1775.

John Hamilton was certainly surrounded on all sides by military family members. He was the son of Captain Silas Hamilton. His brother, Paul, also became a captain. In addition, Paul and John both married daughters of Captain Ezra Stevens. John himself though, may have had an aversion to his own participation in the military during the Revolution. A handwritten contract dated January 1, 1778, and signed by a representative of the Danbury regiment, stated that:

> *This may certify that James Hamilton and John Hamilton, his brother, both of Danbury have this day procured Thomas Shanan (of New Fairfield) an able body man to serve as a soldier during the Present War, in the 2nd Battalion ordered to be raised in the State of Connecticut, Battalion Commanded by Colonel John Dundee, Esq. Certified by me, James Wade, Sergeant, in 2nd Regiment.* [8]

---

[8]   Original document can be found in *Hamilton–Knapp Collection 1742–1924* (Hartford: Connecticut State Library, Archive RG 69:7).

Joseph and John thus appeared to have purchased the service of Thomas Shanan to serve in their stead as a soldier during this time of the Revolution. This, though, was not uncommon.

John Hamilton and Anner Stevens seemed prosperous. At the time of his death in 1803 he owned some 220 acres of land in the area of Bear Mountain. It was parceled out to his children upon his death. He and Anner had five children as follows: [9]

Eli was the eldest son. He was born in 1783, married Hannah Barnum of Danbury on April 16, 1806, and died November 15, 1867. He was a farmer. She was a descendent of one of Danbury's original eight founding families.

Stephen was the second son.

Harvey was the third son.

Jerusha was the eldest daughter.

Cartharina was the younger daughter.

---

9   Children's names from *Distribution of Estate of John Hamilton, December 21, 1804* (Danbury Probate District #2161). These same children's names were re-confirmed in the *Distribution of the Widow's Dower from the Estate of John Hamilton, April 13, 1821* (Danbury Probate). The distribution was the result of the widow, Anner Stevens Hamilton marrying Solomon Glover.

Very little has been discovered about the lives of these children, with the slight exception of Eli Hamilton. The newspaper *Spirit of the Times* reported on March 16, 1831, that a meeting of anti-masonic republicans of the town of Danbury was held at the house of Eli Hamilton on February 28. The group reportedly elected a committee of correspondence, which included Hugh Starr, Lewis R. Starr and Orrin Knapp. [10] This is the first mention of masons relating to the Hamiltons. However, a number of Hamiltons were active masons, including several of Eli's descendents.

Eli and Hannah lived in Danbury and had the following three children:

Norman B. Hamilton was born January 21, 1807, and died of consumption on January 13, 1873. He married Mary

NORMAN B. HAMILTON
(DATE UNKNOWN)

---

10   The *Spirit of the Times* (Bridgeport, CT) Volume: I Issue: 24 Page: 2 as cited by the American Antiquarian Society, 2004 in GenealogyBank.com.

Ann Hopkins of New York. In 1850 he was a farmer according to the census and other official records. They had six children before she died in 1857 in childbirth at the age of 46. Norman then married Martha E. Gates, who was 33 years younger than he. He is buried in Danbury's Pembroke Cemetery with both spouses listed on the same gravestone.

BELIEVED TO BE MARY
ANN HOKPINS (DATE
UNKNOWN)

George Washington Hamilton was born April 19, 1813. He married Laura E. Knapp on June 18, 1843. Laura was born June 21, 1816. They resided in the Pembroke district of Danbury, where George served as judge of probate.[11] They had no children. George was very active in civic life

11   Horace Gillette Cleveland, *Genealogy of Benjamin Cleveland* (Chicago: Horace Gilette Cleveland, 1879), p. 234.

and also accumulated large land holdings in Pembroke. He died June 30, 1892.

Philander was born August 4, 1819, married Betsy Ann Stone on November 24, 1844, and died October 15, 1868, from a spinal ailment. He was a farmer. He is buried in Danbury's Pembroke Cemetery.

CHAPTER THREE

MINNESOTA TERRITORY & CIVIL WAR

(1856–61)

orman B. Hamilton and Mary Ann Hopkins had six children in Danbury as follows:

George Norris Hamilton was born February 5, 1830. He married Mary Eliza Thorpe, and died in August 1901 of organic heart disease.

Edgar H. Hamilton was born April 27, 1832, and died at the age of 13 on July 23, 1845.

Eli Clark Hamilton was born February 3, 1837, married Mary F. Plow on April 8, 1864, and died in Richmond on February 25, 1865.

William H. Hamilton was born March 8, 1840, married Mary J. Hamilton (maiden name unknown), and died on November 20, 1905.

Starr Hamilton was born July 26, 1843. He married Mary Ann Downs. He died in New York on March 27, 1912.

Mary Ardell Hamilton was born January 3, 1857. She died at age 5 on April 22, 1862.

JOUNEY TO MINNESOTA

George Norris Hamilton, known as Norris, was the first-born son, and seems to have played the role of older brother to his much younger siblings. He appears to have had a strong compulsion at an early age to travel out West, to explore new territory, and find the true Wild West for himself. Hence, on March 31, 1856, at the age of 26, he struck out alone to find his fortune. He endured a long journey, and wound up in Minnesota Territory, several years before statehood, years before the cowboys, and roaming amidst Indians and villans. He kept a fairly detailed diary of his journey, the source of this recounting. [1]

Danbury built its first railway connection in 1852. Four years later Norris himself was a passenger. After leaving his girlfriend and future wife, Mary Eliza Thorpe, on the Danbury station platform, he took the train to New York City. He describes in detail how, over several days, he then made his way to Buffalo, and then on to Toledo, Ohio, which

---

1   George Norris Hamilton, from his personal diary, in *Hamilton–Knapp Collection 1742–1924* (Hartford: Connecticut State Library, Archive RG 69:7). Also see Chapter 11 for transcription.

he characterized as "the vilest place I ever saw and the most villainous looking set of men anyone could wish to see." His observations call forth colorful, often humerous images. He describes how his train arrived late in Toledo because the engine detatched from the train cars, and the engineer did not notice the missing cars for five miles. One can only imagine the chaos.

Norris then continued by train to Chicago and Ottawa, Illinois. He described calling on relatives of people who lived in Danbury as he sought work and direction. He traveled back to Chicago, a city which he seemed to like, via Joliet. He later traveled to Rockford, then Dunleith, Illinois, on the Mississippi River, where he boarded the steamboat *Tishomingo* for Winona, Minnesota. He speaks fondly of the captain on the ship. At one point, he reports passing by an Indian encampment with "Red men" earnestly watching the ship "with consternation." He never mentions weapons or actual conflict in his diary.

From Winona, he made his way to Rochester, Minnesota Territory, and from there, he decided to try to stake a land claim. He described a great land rush taking place, with claims being staked many miles out from the then-village of Rochester. However, running low on cash, he was compelled to take up working on a farm for 19 dollars a month. Most days he spent also checking in at the post office, desperate for letters from home. In June 1856 he walked seven miles out of Rochester one day in order to reach some unclaimed land. He eventually found some, and staked his claim. But he was

MINNESOTA 1856, GEORGE NORRIS HAMILTON,
(BELIEVED SEATED FRONT RIGHT)

deeply discouraged by the hardship of it all. He described extreme exhaustion from all the walking.

In early July he attended a "Kansas Meeting," presumably about the ongoing conflict in Kansas over whether its residents would vote to make it a slave state or a free state; partisans on both sides were widely recruited in other states and territories. The Hamiltons seem to have been strong abolitionists.

Subsequently, Norris wrote of becoming sick of farming after only several weeks, and searched around for other things to do. He described being increasingly obsessed with finding a beautiful girl, which he never seemed to achieve. He reported seeing a company of about 20 Indians in full Indian costume on ponies in Rochester near the post office.

In late July 1856 Norris wrote of falling ill worse than he had ever been. But, by July 27 he detailed how he went out in the prairie about 10 miles to "get a girl." But he failed, and wrote that he could not "get her." He was making $20 per month at the time. He took on different jobs, cutting bricks, curing hay, and chopping wood. In early September 1856 he started gathering logs on his claim, hoping to build a hut. However, he soon fell ill again and suffered several bouts of rheumatism. Still, he eventually erected a cabin on his claim. At the end of September he attended a "ball" and actually claimed to have seen "pretty girls." By mid-October he wrote of husking corn for an entire week. On October 20, 1856, he sold his claim. It was clear he was becoming disillusioned with Minnesota.

By November he began planning to leave for a better climate, but was unsure where to go. He described his only option as traveling down the Mississippi by steamship and stopping somewhere new.

On Election Day 1856, Norris lamented that he was unable to vote for "Frémont for Freedom," a reference to rebellious Republican John C. Frémont of California, who was running a campaign vigorously opposed the expansion of slavery into any new states

In mid-December 1856 Norris received news from home, which led him to ponder whether to return. He started heading East out of Minnesota, unsure where he would actually go. However, on December 22 he received three letters from home, and immediately set out for Danbury. He arrived December 27. He never described the catalyst for his hasty return, but his mother died in childbirth on January 3, one week later, at the age of 46. Her child, a girl, survived her, but only to the age of five. Norris seemed relieved but unsure about returning. Still, he was now back with his girlfriend, Mary Eliza Thorpe, whom he married a few years later. The transcription of his entire handwritten journal can be found in Chapter 11.

MARY ELIZA THORPE
APRIL 3, 1852

Despite his apparent dislike of Minnesota farming, Norris subsequently worked as a farmer in the Pembroke area of Danbury. The 1860 birth certificate of his son, Edgar Edward Hamilton, stated that Norris was a farmer. Moreover, according to the local press, on August 7, 1866, Norris was engaged "mowing on his farm" with a scythe. At some point the blade slipped from his hand and cut a bad gash in the fleshy part of the forearm. [2] This was news in 1866.

CIVIL WAR

With the outbreak of the Civil War, the Hamilton family contributed three of its four sons to the mustering of the Connecticut Volunteers: Clark, William, and Starr. With Danbury emerging as a major center for hat production, the three Hamilton brothers claimed at the time to be hatters by profession. Norris remained in Danbury, most likely because he was recently married and his first son was one year old. His brothers all marched off.

Clark enlisted as a private in Averill's Rifles, Company A of the 11th Regiment of Connecticut Volunteers on September 25, 1861, and mustered in on October 24, 1861. [3,4] He was reported a deserter on January 19, 1863. However, one month later Clark was shown as having reenlisted as a private in Battery B of the 5th Artillery Regiment in Mar-

---

2   "State Matters," *Connecticut Courant* (Hartford, CT), Volume CIII, Issue 5299, August 11, 1866, page 1 as found in <http://www.GenealogyBank.com> (September 19, 2015) and copyrighted by NewsBank and/or the American Antiquarian Society 2004.

3   "Muster Roll of the 'Averill Rifles' Company A, 11th Regiment, Connecticut Volunteers," *Danbury Times* (Danbury: December 12, 1861).

4   *Compilation of Civil War Soldiers* (Danbury: Danbury Museum & Historical Society Authority).

tinsburg, Virginia. The reenlistment papers noted that as of February 6, 1863, he was "enlisted" even though the reenlistment papers were dated February 29, 1864. In the section on "Character," Clark was described as "An excellent soldier." [5]

Indeed, the records of battle in the following chapters suggest that Clark was a competent soldier who suffered significantly under the command of the Connecticut 11th Volunteer Regiment. He issued particularly sharp criticisms

BELIEVED TO BE WILLIAM H.
HAMILTON (UNDATED)

---

5   Army of the United States, Re-enlistment Papers of Clark Hamilton, *Hamilton–Knapp Collection 1742–1924* (Hartford: Connecticut State Library, Archive RG 69:7).

of corruption among the officers, some of which became public. It seems that he became so disillusioned during his time with the 11th that he eventually found a way to "desert" without being charged with desertion, by enlisting with a regular (i.e., non-volunteer) regiment. He then continued into battles.

Clark's younger brother, William H. Hamilton, also enlisted as a private in Averill's Rifles, Company A of the 11th Regiment of Connecticut Volunteers on September 15, 1861. He was 21-years-old at the time, and described himself as a farmer. He reenlisted as a veteran on January 1, 1864. He mustered out on December 21, 1865. [6] His military records confirm that he fought in the following battles: Newbern (March 14, 1862), South Mountain (September 14, 1862), Swift Creek (May 10, 1864), Drewry's Bluff (May 16, 1864), Cold Harbor (June 3, 1864), and the siege of Petersburg in 1864. He was in an invalid detachment in the South Street U.S.A. General Hospital in Philadelphia from September 1862 until December 31, 1863. It appears that he was wounded at South Mountain, a Union victory, albeit with high casualties. He was fighting there alongside brother Clark. Nevertheless, there are no indications that he suffered in, or disliked the Connecticut Volunteers Regiment like his brother Clark. Rather, William proudly sported his military affiliation on his gravestone in Pembroke Cemetery. When he mustered out in 1865 he claimed to be a hatter by profession.

---

6   Official U.S. Military Records of William H. Hamilton, *National Archives and Records Administration.*

Youngest brother Starr Hamilton enlisted at the age of nineteen on August 24, 1862, with Company G of the 23rd Regiment. He mustered in on November 14, 1862, for a period of nine months, largely spent around New Orleans. He mustered out on August 31, 1863. [7] Six months later he reenlisted in Company A of the 11th Infantry Regiment of Connecticut Volunteers on February 9, 1864. There he joined brother William, who had sponsored Starr's reenlistment. Starr then fought alongside William in the battles of Swift Creek (May 10, 1864), and Drewry's Bluff (May 16, 1864). He was seriously wounded on June 3, 1864, in the battle of Cold Harbor, Virginia, (where brother William was also fighting). He spent the next five months at Knight U.S.A. General Hospital in New Haven, Connecticut. He returned to his unit in late October, 1864, but by March he was back in the hospital, this time at Fort Monroe, Virginia, due to continued problems from his injuries. [8] He received a disability discharge on September 16, 1865. [9]

Elder brother George Norris Hamilton remained at home during the Civil War and received occasional letters from his three brothers about their whereabouts and the course of the war. These letters are preserved in the *Hamilton–Knapp Collection* in the Connecticut State Library. Clark was the most prolific of the three, and he provided a

---

7   Official U.S. Military Records of Starr Hamilton, *National Archives and Records Administration.*

8   Ibid.

9   *Compilation of Civil War Soldiers* (Danbury: Danbury Museum & Historical Society Authority).

wealth of recountings to add to the growing collection of Hamilton history anecdotes.

CHAPTER FOUR

SHIPWRECKED:
THE BARK *VOLTIGEUR*

*T*he Civil War hit the Hamiltons hard. New anecdotes of living history were shaped by real, and often bitter experience, in many of the most well-known events of the war. Fortunately, a good number of letters from the Hamiltons were preserved, providing some unique flavor. It seems that at the beginning, the Hamiltons were extremely patriotic and even enthusiastic about joining the War of Rebellion. Two of them immediately joined the Connecticut Volunteers in 1861.

According to Lt. Colonel Charles Warren, late of the 11th Connecticut Volunteer Infantry Regiment,

the Eleventh Regiment was organized and mustered into service at Hartford on November 27, 1861, for 3 years service. It remained in camp until December 16 when it was ordered to Annapolis MD. When leaving Hartford, it numbered 927 officers and men. They were led by Colonel THC Kingsbury. A handsome set of regimental colors were presented at New York on December 17,

1861. The regiment encamped at Annapolis and was assigned to Burnside's North Carolina Expedition. On January 1, 1862, they broke camp and boarded ships: half of the regiment boarded the gunboat **Sentinel** *and the other half loaded onto the bark* **Voltigeur**. *The next day after sailing from Fort Monroe, a great storm hit the fleet, which lasted for several days. The* **Voltigeur** *was carried onto the beach at Cape Hatteras. After 29 days on board, the regiment went into camp near Hatteras.* [1]

Clark and William were both part of this group that headed to Annapolis and boarded ships south. Clark was on the bark *Voltigeur* and writes to his brother George Norris

BARK *VOLTIGEUR*

---

[1]   Lt. Colonel Charles Warren, *"History of the Eleventh Connecticut Volunteer Infantry Regiment."* Warren served with the 11th CVI. His three-page undated history is found at <http://www.11thcvi.org/files/11th_history.pdf> (18 September 2015).

Hamilton on February 1, 1862, the following: [2]

On Board the Barque Voltigeur
shipwrecked on the beach
Hatteras Inlet
February 1, 1862

Brother Norris,

I received the papers you sent and also the letter you wrote Bill. I don't wonder that you are inclined to blame us for not writing before this but I will try and give you a faint idea of what we have encountered since leaving Annapolis and then you can judge for yourself whether we were to blame or not. We left our encampment at Annapolis on the morning of the 7th of January and marched down to the dock where we were obliged to stand around until after dark before we could board. We finally got started, however, and got on board about 9 o'clock. The right wing on this ship, and the left on another. We took up our quarters in the hold of the ship. We were packed in pretty close. There is hardly room enough to turn around when they are all out of their bunks. We lay in the harbor until the 9th, when the fleet began to make preparations for leaving. Vessel after vessel passed us loaded with troops with the stars and stripes flying

---

2   Transcription of original letter from the *Hamilton–Knapp Collection 1742–1924* (Hartford: Connecticut State Library, Archive RG 69:7).

at the masthead and each one with their bands playing Dix-
ieland. The sight was an exhilarating one, I assure you.

At last we were taken in tow in company with the
New York Zouaves. Everything went smoothly enough until
about 9 o'clock in the evening when crash went something
against the vessel which almost throwed us out of our bunks.
It seems that the vessel ahead, owing to the carelessness of
the pilot, ran aground, and our vessel ran into her. Fortunately there was not much damage done. We cast anchor
and lay there for about two days waiting for the steamer to
get off. But she couldn't raise it. So the captain finally made
sail and started off without them. We arrived off fortress
Munroe on Saturday night where we found the fleet ready to
sail. We had orders to sail in an hour after we arrived but we
were out of water and had to wait till morning to take in a
supply. We got ready about 10 the next morning and started.
We were soon outside of Cape Henry and bounding away
on the ocean. The weather was very rough, with a heavy sea
running, and continued so until we came in sight of Cape
Hatteras.

On the 16th we struck one of the shoals the same day
and came very near being wrecked, but we got off safe and
anchored outside of the breakers. The next day a pilot boat
came out and showed us the way in but we struck several
times coming over the bar but without doing much damage.
We finally over and anchored where we supposed we were
safe but on the 21st a terrible gale came up and the vessel
dragged anchor and we expected every minute to go on the
breaks, in which case every man would have been lost. The

captain was obliged to run the vessel on to the beach in order to save the lives of the men. It was for a long time doubtful whether he would succeed in doing it. We had the flag of distress up for two days but no help came to us and the vessel is a wreck.

High and dry on the beach and no lives lost, we went ashore on the 21st for the first time since leaving Annapolis and rambled all over the island. It is the most God forsaken place I ever saw. We found a few cattle and horses. How they live here is a mystery to me. Some of the boys killed 3 or 4 and had a feast but I didn't want any such meat. For me there is plenty of clams here and we are having good times again, nothing to do but run about the island in the day time and come back to the ship at night to sleep. What we are staying here so long for the lord only knows for I don't.

February 10

When I commenced this letter I expected to send it the same day but the mail steamer left before I could get it ready so I thought I would wait until I had another chance to write. The fleet finally sailed and left us. And we were ordered to cross the inlet and go into camp, which we did. We were taken off ...*illegible*... on the then 7th and put on board a schooner where we stayed all night and boarded the next morning and embarked to press about. On the 7th morning and marched to present ...*illegible*... about two miles maybe ...*illegible*... in a grove of live oak and underbrush. We had to go work and make the ground to pitch our tents, but we have got settled down pretty comfortably now. If the sun would only shine once in a while, it would seem quite like home again.

We have heard that the fleet have been successful, but have not heard the particulars yet. I suppose you will hear from it long before we do, as we don't hear no more what is going on than if we were out of world hardly. I wish you would send a New York paper once in a while. You must not stop writing because you don't hear from us very often, as we don't very often have a chance to send a letter. There is no such thing as buying a postage stamp here, so I have to get my letters franked. If you think you can send me a dollar's worth and have them come safe, I wish you would. And you can take your pay out of the next money I send home.

> Yours,
> Clark Hamilton

Company A Connecticut 11th Regiment C V Burnsides Division, Hatteras Inlet, North Carolina

———————

At this early phase of the war, Clark reflects a certain enthusiasm that seemed widespread among many of the enlistees. However, the hardships of just getting near rebel forces were significant. A comprehensive history of the

Connecticut 11th Volunteers by Croffut and Morris, notes that in late January 1862, only 72 of 120 boats which had left Fort Monroe, survived the sea journey south. They note that the bark *Voltigeur* lay beached for 23 days before the vessel "went to pieces." [3]

However, preparations continued for the next weeks for the battle of New Bern. Clark and William were both there.

---

3   Croffut, W. A., and John M. Morris. *The Military and Civil History of Connecticut During the War of 1861–65* (New York: Ledyard Bill, 1868), p. 164.

CHAPTER FIVE

BATTLE OF NEW BERN

(1862)

*A*ccording to Warren's history of the Connecticut 11th Volunteers,

early in March 1862, the regiment next moved to Roanoke Island and joined the forces preparing to oper- ate against Newbern. The regiment had an active part in the attack on Newbern, being near the center of the line and in the final charge their colors were among the foremost on the enemy's works. After the battle, the reg- iment encamped on the Trent until July, when it was ordered to join the Army of the Potomac at Fredericks- burg, VA and was placed on duty in that city. [1]

The battle of New Bern took place on March 14, 1862. Clark Hamilton writes to his brother George Norris Hamil-

---

1   Lt. Colonel Charles Warren, *History of the Eleventh Con- necticut Volunteer Infantry Regiment.* Warren served with the 11th CVI. His three-page undated history can be found at <www.11thcvi. org/files/11th_history.pdf> (September 18, 2015).

ton that very day after the battle as follows: [2]

———————

Newbern, N.C.
March 14, 1862

In my last letter to our folks I wrote that we had left Roanoke Island and gone on board a steamer. We left there the 11th and arrived opposite the mainland on the Neuse river early yesterday morning, and commenced landing our troops, which took until about 4 o'clock in the afternoon, when we commenced our march upon the enemy's battery, which is about 15 or 20 miles from the place where we landed. We came to a halt about 10 o'clock, about 5 miles from the enemy position, where we stayed all night and commenced our march upon them this morning. And after a hard-fought battle we drove them from their position and Newbern is ours.

Me and Bill and all the rest of the Pembroke boys escaped without a scratch. Our regiment suffered severely. The loss in killed and wounded is not known yet. There is 14 of our company missing; 3 or 4 are known to be wounded and the rest we have not heard from. I had 2 or 3 narrow escapes. One ball came close to my face and struck the man

———————

[2]   Transcription of original letter from the *Hamilton–Knapp Collection 1742–1924* (Hartford: Connecticut State Library, Archive RG 69:7).

behind me in the shoulder and wounded him dangerous-ly. Dave Mansfield had a loud call also. A ball struck his blankets, which he had strung on his shoulder and lodged in the blankets without hurting him. The shot and shell flew like hailstones about us for a spell. I tell you the rebel force was about 9,000 and strongly fortified. Ours were about the same with the addition of the gunboats on the river. After we drove them out of the batteries, they retreated back to the city, which they fired before we could catch up with them. And the city is now all in flames. How many we captured, I have not yet learned as we have only just arrived here - but it is a large number, they say.

Our boys are having a good time picking up things, which they left in their flight. I have got tobacco enough to last me 9 months and other things too numerous to mention. Bill is in his glory as he found a nice bugle to blow on. This is an important victory as it commands the railroad running north and south. I think it will wind up the war in North Carolina. I hope so at any rate. I have been in one battle and I am satisfied it is a hard sight to look upon the dead and dy-ing. I have written this in a hurry because I knew you would be anxious to know whether we were safe or not. I will write the particulars next time. I received a letter from our folks the day before we landed, and they say Bill Penly told them that Bill was sick in the hospital at Annapolis. Now a more damnable lie was never told. He never was in the hospital at Annapolis nor any other hospital. And to make things sure, he will write a few lines with this and satisfy you that it is false. And if that ain't enough, I will get the rest of the Pembroke boys to prove it beyond dispute. I believe I have nothing more to say this time and have had a hard day's work and feel pretty tired. Write as soon as you get this.

Yours,
Clark Hamilton

I have heard that Bill Penly stated that I was sick in Annapolis, but I have not been. I have had a hard fight today so I won't write more. Tell Bill that he is a damn liar.

William H. Hamilton

P.S. I received your papers that you sent. Do so some more. This letter is written on search paper, captured in their camp, which we now occupy.

Yours,
C. Hamilton

———————

Croffut and Morris report that the Connecticut 11th suffered six men killed, including a captain, and 14 wounded that day. [3] Though the Connecticut 11th distinguished itself admirably in the battle of New Bern, it appears to have had certain disciplinary challenges that would become clearer over the coming months, with Clark playing a role of antagonist.

During the late spring of 1862 Clark and William remained around New Bern, North Carolina. In May, Clark wrote home concerning the death of his five-year-old sister Mary Ardell Hamilton as follows: [4]

Newbern, N.C.
May 2, 1862

Brother Norris,

I received your letter last night containing the afflicting news of little sis' death. It was sad news for us but we must bear up under it as well as we can. I was in hopes that I should have seen her again alive and well but God has willed

----

3   Croffut, W. A., and John M. Morris. *The Military and Civil History of Connecticut During the War of 1861–65* (New York: Ledyard Bill, 1868), p. 175.

4   Transcription of original letter from the *Hamilton–Knapp Collection 1742–1924* (Hartford: Connecticut State Library, Archive RG 69:7).

it otherwise and we must bow to his will although it is hard to think that we never shall see her again in this world. We were unprepared for such news. We did not know that she had been sick until we received your letter last night. Little did I dream before I opened your letter, of the sad news, which it contained. I can write no more this time. Write and let me know how Grandfather and Betsy Ann are getting along. I will write again in a few days. Bill wants to know who wrote him the note he received with yours as there is no name signed to it.

Yours,
Clark Hamilton

———————

A week later Clark writes home to complain about the miserable lot of a soldier's life: [5]

———————

Newbern,
May 8, 1862

———————

5   Ibid.

Brother Norris,

I received your letter of the 27th this morning and I was glad to hear from home once more. It is hard for us to realize that our little sister is no more that. If we are ever spared to go home again, she will not be there to greet us with her merry laugh. I was in hopes that she could have been spared, but it was not so to be and we must bear up under this great affliction the best we can. Bill Loeach has gone home today on a furlough of 20 days. He has been very sick and is going home to recruit up. I wish we were all going for I am getting tired and sick of a soldier's life.

A soldier's life is a hard one at the best, but it is made a great deal harder for us than there is any necessity for. Our officers take no interest in our welfare. Whether we get anything to eat or not is all the same to them so long as they get what they want. The consequence is, the quartermaster is robbing the regiment every day. If we hadn't had the good fortune to find plenty of frying pans and kettles in the rebel camp, which we occupied when we first came to Newbern, I don't know what we should have done. For more than a week the quartermaster didn't weigh out a thing to us, and we had to live on the provisions the rebels left. But there was plenty of it and we cooked hasty puddings and pancakes and got along pretty well as long as it lasted. We are all getting to be great cooks. When we get sick of salt-horse we go to the settlers and buy some mackerel or codfish and potatoes and have a good meal. Fresh fish are plenty here, and cheap, and the best I ever ate.

Enclosed you will find a bounty check of ten dollars. I wish you would draw the money on it and send us a box of things. I would like some cheese and dried beef, and a few pickles and such things. Also a couple of handkerchiefs apiece for us, and some combs and a couple of towels - for these are articles that we cannot get here. If you could send us some wine, it would come very acceptable. Send us these things and whatever else you are a mind to by express and take your pay with the ten dollars. I don't know as I have anything more to write. The Pembroke boys are all pretty well. I have been rather unwell for a few days but I am getting better. Now Bill's ...*illegible*... have got entirely well.

Yours,
C. Hamilton

P.S. One thing I forgot to mention. I want some envelopes and paper. I shall also send Bill's bounty with this if he has it made out in time. He has had two made out and both were wrong. I hope he will get one right this time. Write and let us know whether you received the money we sent home about the 9th of April. C.H.

———

Clark's May lament came at a time where others were starting to notice a substantial breakdown in the structure of the Connecticut 11th Regiment of Volunteers. Croffut and Morris even assert that during this time the 11th was "the most disorderly and slovenly" regiment in the division.[6] Quite a broad condemnation.

By June a demoralized Clark seems to be showing the stress of long waiting and poor administration of the military. His criticism of the 11th Regiment, his superiors and the Union cause grows. [7]

———————

Newbern, N.C.
June 24, 1862

Brother Norris,

I once more take my I was going to say pen but it happens to be a pencil in hand to write you a few lines to let you know what is going on here as far as I know and that isn't much. Today we hear that four companies of our regiment, among which is Company A, are ordered to leave here to-

———————

6   Croffut, W. A., and John M. Morris. *The Military and Civil History of Connecticut During the War of 1861–65* (New York: Ledyard Bill, 1868), p. 257.

7   Transcription of original letter from the *Hamilton–Knapp Collection 1742–1924* (Hartford: Connecticut State Library, Archive RG 69:7).

morrow on a skirmishing expedition. Up the country several regiments fell here a day or two ago and one of them has
come back and they report a considerable force of the rebels
somewhere between here and Goldsboro, S.C. We stand a
pretty good chance of having a brush with the rebels before
long; that is if they don't run as they generally do.

Burnside has been receiving large reinforcements
of cavalry and for the past two weeks. So he is pretty well
prepared for them. Our chaplain has returned from the
North, where he has been on furlough. And today we have
had preaching. For the first time since leaving Hatteras, the
regiment was turned out under arms and compelled to go
whether they wanted to or not. It caused a great dissatisfac-
tion among the men, but they can't help themselves. We are
under a despotism more galling than that of the niggers, who
are the cause of this accursed war. But we have got to grin
and bear it. It can't last always. However, some of us will see
the day probably, when we shall be our own masters again.
We hope to see the time, when we can lay down at night
without the infernal sound of the drum to call us to roll call
at 9 o'clock at night and 6 in the morning, or standing guard
24 hours rain or shine. We are not even considered to know
whether we are sick and unfit for duty or not but we must go
to the doctor's. But we must go to the doctor's, and if he sees
fit, he can excuse us and give us some medicine. Otherwise
we must drill whether we are able to stand up or not.

But I guess I have said about enough to give you some
idea of the way we live. I feel a little out of humor today, but
I guess I will get over it. I can say to you and levi that you

done the wisest thing you ever done when you didn't enlist in the 11th regiment, for I believe it is the worst officered and worst managed regiment that ever left the state of Connecticut or any other state for the honor of the union. I hope there is not any more like it. One thing I am pretty sure of, if I ever get out of this to use the language of Rus. Smith in his letter to the Times, this glorious union can go to the devil for all me. Our chaplain did not talk very encouraging to us today about our going home very soon says he the people in Connecticut when they got the news of the recent victories would congratulate themselves on the prospect of our return in the course of a few weeks but, says he, don't flatter yourselves with any such prospect. Instead of weeks it will take years to bring the rebels again back to their lawful government. Well, never mind, if it is three years let it be three years. There is one consolation about it - they have only 9 months more to exercise their power over us, our officers I mean, and then we shall be as good as they are.

May 19th

Hearing last night that a mail had arrived, I postponed closing this letter until this morning when I received your letter of the 9th and was glad to hear from you and that our folks were getting better. Another mail came in this morning but will not be distributed before night. The report about our leaving today turns out like 99 stories out of a hundred that we hear to be a false report. I suppose it started from the fact that two companies C and H are ordered out two or three miles from camp to do picket duty. I guess it is about time to close this letter. The weather is hotter than a niggers nest with the old nigger on the boys are all well.

Clark Hamilton

————————

Against the backdrop of growing disgruntlement in these letters, Clark and Norris did not shy from going public. On May 18, 1862 the *Danbury Times* printed almost verbatim most of the text of Clark's letter to Norris of May 8, including his bitter complaints about the regiment's leadership and quartermaster. [8] The *Times* attributed the anonymous text to "Under date of Newbern May 8th, 1862, a Danbury volunteer writes." Norris had clearly shared Clark's May 8 letter (with or without Clark's permission) with the *Times*. Significantly the *Times* then added its own blistering endorsement to Clark's complaints, stating that: [9]

The source from whence the above comes is conclusive to us that the complaint would not be made without cause. With ample arrangements made for provisioning the troops, it is clear enough to be seen that whatever is withheld from the mouths of the soldiers goes

8   Anonymous Letter, *Danbury Times*, May 18, 1862.

9   Editorial comment to Anonymous Letter, *Danbury Times*, May 18, 1862.

into the pockets of government officials, in some di-rection, and that they are thus enabled to fatten at the expense of the hungry soldiers does not "go down" in this quarter: Throwing justice and humanity entirely out of the question, we are warned that the cause of the Union is not yet beyond the need of honest and brave soldiers, and policy alone would indicate that it were worse than madness to allow them to be thus straight-ened in regard to their rations. A check sent with the above will be duly invested as the boys wish, and if the inconvenience they experience is more than tem-porary, they will know where they will find supplies.

This appears to have set off quite a controversy over corruption by the officers in Company A of the Eleventh Connecticut Volunteers Infantry Regiment. At least one person then stood up publicly against Clark in support of Company A. On June 18, 1862, the *Jeffersonian* published a May 31, 1862, letter from a soldier with the initials G.D.F. under the title "A Misstatement Corrected." The letter effu-sively praises the officers and supplies of Company A as the best, and criticizes harshly the author (Clark) of the *Dan-bury Times* May 8 letter. GDF writes, in part: [10]

Now let me give you some facts as to that week and how we fared. Co. A was landed at the mouth of Slocum's Creek, on the afternoon of the 13th of March. The day before the battle...Maj. Stedman came up and told us that provisions had been landed, and advised all that

10   G.D.F., "A Misstatement Corrected," *Jeffersonian*, June 18, 1862.

had not got their three days' rations in their haversacks, to get them then. Capt. Southmayd advised the same; they were told by the company that we had already got a supply, and the company refused to go back to the landing to get more, the Captain remarking that if we had not enough, it would be our own fault and we ought not to complain. The battle was fought on Friday, and won, and our regiment quartered in the barracks of the flying rebels; we there found the frying pans and kettles the writer speaks of, with plenty of bacon and corn-meal...Lieutenant Bailey and White took a squad of men, myself among the number, on Sunday after the battle, out to one of these plantations, and we brought in over a hundred weight of chickens, besides some geese and ducks; they were dressed, cooked and served out to the whole company. Mules and carts were sent out, and sweet potatoes and turnips brought in by the cart load and served out to the regiment, of which Co. A receieved its share...I saw no lack of interest in our welfare, on the part of our officers...I can't see how this poor hungry soldier, nearly two months after the battle, happens to wake up and write this silly letter. If he did not have enough to eat, I believe it was because he was to lazy to get it. It is certainly too bad that our wives, fathers, mothers and children should be tormented with fears that we are starving. I can bear testimony to the uniform kindness of Capt. Southmayd and his other officers. Their conduct has been such to me, and I have never known them to neglect or abuse others. Perhaps the gentlemen that makes complaint, belives what he writes, but I believe his wrongs are more imaginery than real.

The sharp tone of the response to Clark's letter is indicative that the issue of rations and corruption in Company A was boiling over. It also makes clear that the officers of Company A would have to be looking for the author of the *Danbury Times* letter, if they did not already know that it was Clark.

After digesting the *Jeffersonian* article and rebuke of his complaints, Clark writes to his brother, Norris, in late June. Clark tries again to describe the up close reality for the soldier, but also to point out that the soldier who wrote the *Jeffersonian* letter was a hypocrite because he numbered among one of the most vocal critics of the regiment's officers.[11]

———————

Newbern, N.C.
June 24, 1862

Brother Norris,

Having received the papers you sent, and noticing an asterisk in the Jeffersonian of the 18th which calls in question

———————

11   Transcription of original letter from the *Hamilton–Knapp Collection 1742–1924* (Hartford: Connecticut State Library, Archive RG 69:7).

my veracity for truth telling, I thought I would not let the opportunity pass of saying a few words in my own defense. The
article in question is headed a misstatement corrected now. I
think if the writer had headed it a correct statement misstat-
ed, it would have been more appropriate, for he knows that
what he states is with one or two exceptions an unmitigated
falsehood which he says in regard to our landing at Slocum's
Creek and refusing to take provisions with us is true, he then
goes on to state of our fight of the next day and taking up our
quarters in the deserted barracks of the rebels. Now these
barracks were the horse stables of the rebel cavalry and we
had to remove the manure before they were fit to sleep in. It
is also true that there was some poultry brought into camp of
which we had one good meal. But as to sweet potatoes and
turnips being brought in by cartloads, they must have exist-
ed in the writer's imagination, for I saw neither. (Nor) can I
find anyone who did see sweet potatoes and turnips come in
by the cartload. He says that it is singular; I should wait two
months after the battle and write this silly letter. If he had a
little more sense, he would see that I did not find fault with
the living while the provisions of the rebels lasted; on the
contrary, I was perfectly satisfied. It was not until after we
had changed our camp that I was anyways disconcerted with
the living, and then it did not last long.

Now this very same writer who is so loud in the praises of our officers has been one of the loudest in his denun-
ciations of our treatment. And no longer than yesterday, I
heard him condemning the conduct of the officers towards
the privates. And yet he comes out in his letter and says he
has never seen any neglect on the part of the officers. Oh

consistency, thou art indeed a jewel. I have written this for the purpose of justifying myself from his unprovoked attack upon me. And perhaps my statement, supported as it can be by three-fourths of the men in the company, is entitled to as much credit as his, which is regarded by the whole company with that contempt which the low groveling tone of the article deserves.

Yours,
C. Hamilton

———————

In early July, 1862, the Connecticut 11th Regiment moved to Newport News. Croffut and Morris describe a reorganization of the "field and line" of the regiment. They note: [12]

> It's lieutenant-colonel, a noble and patriotic man, but not of a military turn of mind, had resigned at Newberne; and its colonel, who had never much loved or adorned the service, here also took final leave of the regiment.... The new colonel daily drilled the battalion in the strictest manner. Severe inspections also began. A spot of

———————

12   Croffut, W. A., and John M. Morris. *The Military and Civil History of Connecticut During the War of 1861–65* (New York: Ledyard Bill, 1868), p. 257.

dirt secured a reprimand, and an unclean musket was a sure passport to extra duty or the guard-house. No man was allowed to step out of his company-street unless his coat was on, and every button buttoned. There was fierce commotion for a time, and smothered threats of mutiny; but the colonel was master, and, within the three weeks of stay at Newport News, the regiment improved beyond description....Thenceforward, for three years, the Eleventh had few if any superiors.

It appears that Clark's laments, and those of others, may have been heard, even though the officers praised by Clark's detractor were not those identified by Coffit and Morris as the officers being replaced.

CHAPTER SIX

BATTLE OF ANTIETAM CREEK

(1862)

*T*he battle of Antietam was among the most renowned of the Civil War. William was wounded at the battle of South Mountain, three days before Antietam. He was hospitalized. However, Clark Hamilton participated in the Antietam clash.

According to Warren, in July 1862,

the regiment was ordered to join the Army of the Potomac at Fredericksburg, VA and was placed on duty in that city. The last of August the regiment evacuated the city, crossed the Rappahannock and burning bridges, moved north to Washington to join the army under McClellan for the Maryland Campaign. They were assigned to Harland's Brigade, in the Ninth Corps. This brigade was in the advance towards Fredrick, and on the 12th of Sept. the skirmish line of the 11th entered the city on the heels of the rebel army. The advance was resumed on the 13th and the rebels were forced back to Turner's Gap at South Mountain, where a desperate battle took place in the late afternoon on the next day. The 11th was under fire but its loss was small. The advance was resumed on the 15th and 16th, when the enemy was found concentrated behind Antietam Creek. The Battle of Antietam commenced early on the 17th and in the afternoon the 11th was in the advance on the left for the capture of the stone bridge. Two companies were detached as skirmishers under Captain Griswold, and plunged into the creek. It was a literal "valley of death." Captain Griswold was killed mid-stream and Colonel Kingsbury was mortally wounded. But the regiment held its ground until supported, when a general charge across the bridge was ordered and drove the rebels from the stone wall and the heights beyond. The 11th lost 181, including every field officer. Being nearly

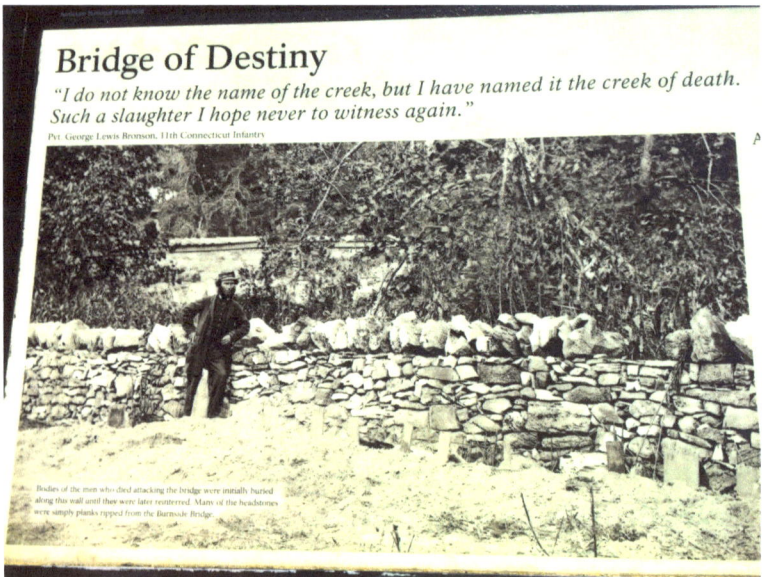

Bridge of Destiny
"I do not know the name of the creek, but I have named it the creek of death. Such a slaughter I hope never to witness again."
Pvt. George Lewis Bronson, 11th Connecticut Infantry

Bodies of the men who died attacking the bridge were initially buried along this wall until they were later reinterred. Many of the headstones were simply planks ripped from the Burnside Bridge.

PLAQUE AT ANTIETAM BURNSIDE'S BRIDGE 2013

out of ammunition, it was relieved but before its boxes could be filled it was again called up to support a battery with the bayonet. The enemy being repulsed and falling back across the Potomac, the regiment went into camp at Pleasant Valley MD. Lt. Colonel Stedman was promoted to Colonel of the regiment. [1]

Clark laments in an October 1 letter to brother Norris the terrible supply conditions in the army. He then describes how he experienced the famous battle of Antietam Creek, which, unlike President Lincoln, he is reluctant to view as a victory. He notes that his brother William is in the hospital nearby. [2] In fact, William had been wounded in the September 14 battle of South Mountain, while fighting alongside Clark.

Near Harpers Ferry, Virginia
October 1, 1862

---

1   Lt. Colonel Charles Warren, *History of the Eleventh Connecticut Volunteer Infantry Regiment.* Warren served with the 11th CVI. His three-page undated history can be found at <www.11thcvi.org/files/11th_history.pdf> (September 18, 2015).

2   Transcription of original letter from the *Hamilton–Knapp Collection 1742–1924* (Hartford: Connecticut State Library, Archive RG 69:7).

Brother Norris,

Having at last an opportunity of writing a few lines, I thought I would improve it by giving you some information of our whereabouts. I suppose you have been wondering at my long silence and blaming me for neglect in not writing before but I will try and give you some idea of the way we have been treated since leaving Washington and then you can judge for yourself whether I could have done better or not. We left Washington on ...*illegible*... marching order. That is, all that we were allowed to take with us besides our guns and accouterments were our rubber and woolen blankets. Our knapsacks were left behind and we have not seen them since. Consequently, I have been out of paper ever since and without means of procuring any more until this morning, when I was lucky enough to get this sheet from the orderly. And I prepared to write you a faint idea of the rascally and inhuman treatment we have received since leaving Washington.

When we left we were in a half-starved condition having barely enough to eat to keep soul and body together. Yet whether it will be believed or not we were actually on the point of starvation in sight of the capital of this great and glorious government, for the preservation of which we are imperiling our lives and suffering all manner or hardships. What in God's name does our government mean by such kind of treatment? Here we are in a land of plenty and actually suffering for the necessaries of life. If they would only pay us off, which they should have done a month ago, we would very soon better our condition. But no, they seem to delight in making our conditions as miserable as possible. We have been four weeks without a change of clothes and no prospect of ever getting any as I see. How long this state of things is to go on I don't know, but it is my impression that if something is not done pretty soon, the soldiers will take things in their own hands. You may perhaps think that I am drawing it pretty strong, but I have not told the half of what we have undergone since leaving Fredericksburg. I have kept still long enough. I have been hoping against hope for better times, until forbearance has ceased to be a virtue. I notice in the Tribune of September 22 a statement from our regimental quartermaster, Lieutenant Davis, which says that our regiment fought all day long at the battle of Antietam without food or drink, which is true. And if he had said that for 2 or 3 weeks previous we had had little or nothing, it would have been true also.

As you have doubtless heard pretty much all the particulars of that battle, I will not attempt to give any general description of it further than of what came under my own observation. Early on that morning the rebels commenced shelling us from the position we had taken the night previous, and soon made it too hot for us there. And we accordingly changed our position for one less exposed, not however before several out of our brigade were killed and wounded. Our artillery were soon brought to bear upon the rebels, and under cover of its fire our regiment was ordered to advance to the bridge and carry it. Companies A and B were ordered to advance as skirmishers to the creek, which we did being met by a tremendous fire from the enemy, which we returned with interest — our sharps rifles doing good execution as the ground afterwards testified. It was here that Captain Griswold fell mortally wounded. He had jumped into the creek waist deep calling on us to follow when he was instantly struck by a rifle shot from the hands a sharpshooter. Probably seeing it to be madness for us to attempt to follow, he called to us to secrete ourselves and made his way across to the opposite side. We then secreted ourselves the best we could, and continued our firing until our ammunition was exhausted.

A Divided Nation–A Divided Family

Union Col. Henry W. Kingsbury (left) and Confederate Gen. David R. Jones (right) married sisters Eva and Rebecca Taylor. At Antietam, Col. Kingsbury, described as a "brilliant, honorable and brave soldier," commanded the 11th Connecticut Infantry that made the first attack on Burnside Bridge. Gen. Jones was nicknamed "Neighbor"Jones for his friendly, outgoing personality. Gen. Jones and the soldiers of his division defended the bridge.

While leading his men, Col. Kingsbury was wounded four times, "suffered great pain during the dressing of his wounds, and survived but twenty-four hours." Four months later, Jones, whose soldiers had killed his brother-in-law, died of a heart attack at age thirty seven.

PLAQUE AT ANTIETAM BURNSIDE'S BRIDGE 2013

In the meantime the bridge had been carried and the rebels driven back, not however, without a great loss of life, our colonel receiving four wounds, one of which proved mortal. Major Moegling was badly wounded in his leg. It is surprising that our company met with so small a loss, only two being wounded besides our captain. After the fighting at the bridge had ceased, we regained our regiment. And after getting a fresh supply of ammunition, we prepared for another encounter with the enemy, they having received large reinforcements during the day, and our troops were having hot work with them over the hill. And we were ordered up to their support, but were finally obliged to fall back as they greatly outnumbered us, and were pouring in destructive cross fires on each side of us which cut us up fearfully.

BURNSIDE'S BRIDGE AT ANTIETAM CREEK 2013
(VIEWED FROM UNION SIDE OF CREEK)

Night finally came on and we barely held our own. How we escaped annihilation I can't see. In the last charge, our Lieutenant-Colonel was wounded and we were left without a field officer.

Thus ended the battle of Antietam creek. It is called a great victory. Well, perhaps it is, but it is a dear bought one, and I cannot help asking myself whether the results obtained by it will compensate for the terrible sacrifice of human life. That we had reinforcements to the number of 80 or 40,000 men right back of us is well known. The question is why they were not brought to our support. Why were one or two brigades allowed to fight against the whole combined force of the rebels? Yet, so it was. To my mind there is gross mismanagement somewhere. We unquestioningly had force enough to demolish entire rebel army, and yet they were allowed their own time to get away, with no decisive results gained on our side. I tell you the soldiers are getting sick of this kind of work.

I would like to write more but I have no space. I wish you would answer this as soon as you get it and send me some money, say 5 dollars, which you can take out of the bank. Direct your letters Clark Hamilton, Company A, 11th Regiment, Connecticut Volunteers, 9th Army Corps, Washington, D.C. and they will come directly through. I have received all your letters and papers at different times on the way. I suppose you know that Bill is in the hospital somewhere between here and Frederick. Do not be alarmed about him as he is in good hands.

Yours,
Clark Hamilton

––––––––––

Clark's hand-wringing over the deployment of Union forces at Antietam reflects that of other observers. Despite the Union "victory," the Connecticut 11th suffered 38 dead and 97 wounded. Clark was unsure who really won. However, his continuing focus on rations and starvation was an ominous harbinger of things yet to come.

CHAPTER SEVEN

BATTLE OF FREDERICKSBURG

(1862–1863)

*A*ccording to Warren,

> *the 11th Connecticut then moved November 5, 1862 across the Potomac at Berlin and marched south until the 9th, when Burnside assumed command and the direction changed to Falmouth, which was reached on November 19th. The brigade camped on Stafford Hills until December 12th when it moved across the river into the city and lay down in the streets waiting for the morrow.* [1]

Clark writes to Norris on December 4 outside Fredericksburg, Virginia to vent displeasure with the slow progress of the war and the abysmal conditions of the soldiers. He views the army leadership as cursed with scoundrels. [2]

---

1   Lt. Colonel Charles Warren, *History of the Eleventh Connecticut Volunteer Infantry Regiment.* Warren served with the 11th CVI. His three-page undated history can be found at <www.11thcvi.org/files/11th_history.pdf> (September 18, 2015).

2   Transcription of original letter from the *Hamilton–Knapp*

———————

Dec 4, 1862
Camp Opposite Fredericksburg, Virginia

Brother Norris,

I once more squat myself for the purpose of giving you some information of how we are getting along. There has been no movement of any importance since I wrote you last. The two armies still stand facing each other on the banks of the Rappahannock and both are seemingly making preparations for a grand battle but both seem unwilling to open the ball. What is to make of it? I don't know. The rebels have been throwing up earthworks back of the city and our forces have been doing the same on this side? What will be the result? Time will tell. One thing I am convinced of and have been for a long time that is that other means than fighting will have to be resorted to before peace will ever be restored. The rebellion, in my opinion, could and should have been suppressed at least six months ago but through the treachery and blundering inefficiency of our leaders the opportunity was lost and thousands of lives have been sacrificed in vain. Justice and humanity demand that this barbarous and inhu-

Collection 1742–1924 (Hartford: Connecticut State Library, Archive RG 69:7).

man war should cease and I hope something will be done by Congress towards settling it without further bloodshed.

Since my last we have moved our camp a little further back on to a dryer and warmer location and are making our quarters as comfortable as we can but they are miserable enough at the best. We have the small shelter tent - one for every two men and they are about as much protection from the weather as a common toadstool would be. The weather is about as cold for all I see as it is in Connecticut at this time of the year. It makes me mad to read the accounts of the lying reporters in the papers about the soldiers being in such good spirits and comfortable quarters and such stuff. One would think to read their accounts that a soldier was the happiest being in existence and that the continuance of the war would be his greatest desire. I saw a statement in the paper today that the army today is but little if any larger than it was before the new levy was called out. But it says nothing of the reason of this if they want to know the reason. Let them ask the private soldier. If government expects to keep men in service let it treat them as men. If a different course is not pursued there will be less interested in …*illegible*… men.

Our army is cursed with the most infamous and contemptible set of scoundrels that ever went unhung and the soldiers are getting tired of being tyrannized over by such things. They care no more for the welfare of the men under their command than they would for a pack of hops. But what high there will be remembered when these soldiers get home tobacco. We scarce here and can be sold readily at three or four dollars a pound. I hope you will send me some in way.

I spoke of when we reserved our knapsacks a few days and I shall try and write a little oftener now.

C. Hamilton

————————

Clark's growing critique of the military seems to continue it's ascent, as the nation girds for growing battles.

Warren recounts that upon the lifting of the fog the morning of December 13,

the Battle of Fredericksburg began and raged until dark. Harland's brigade was not closely engaged with the enemy. The 11th supported the pickets connecting the line of Sumner with Franklin on the left. Their loss was small. General Burnside decided to renew the attack the next day by putting himself at the head of his old corps (the Ninth) and the 11th was selected to lead the advance. He was at last dissuaded from the desperate scheme and the regiment was saved. The Connecticut brigade quietly crossed the pontoons on the night of the 14th and returned to their camps. February 6, 1863 it moved to Newport News, where it remained until March 13. At this place the Connecticut brigade was noted for its fine appearance on parade. [3]

On January 10, 1863, Clark writes about his brothers William and Starr, before ranting again about the scoundrels who are running the army. [4]

————————

Opposite Fredericksburg, Virginia

Brother Norris,

I received your letter of the 1st and was surprised to learn that you had received no letter from me since the battle as I had written and mailed a letter to you a few days after the battle and had been looking for an answer for some time. I got your letter with the twenty shillings worth of postage currency and also one newspaper with a plug of tobacco but as we have been paid off you need not send the remainder at

3   Lt. Colonel Charles Warren, *History of the Eleventh Connecticut Volunteer Infantry Regiment.* Warren served with the 11th CVI. His three-page undated history can be found at <www.11thcvi.org/files/11th_history.pdf> (September 18, 2015).

4   Transcription of original letter from the *Hamilton–Knapp Collection 1742–1924* (Hartford: Connecticut State Library, Archive RG 69:7).

present unless you have already done so. I was glad to hear that you had heard from Bill but I should have been better pleased to have heard of his discharge. However, he had reason to be thankful that he is as well off as he is. I suppose Starr is down in the neighborhood of New Orleans about this time. Well, I hope he never will have to suffer the hardships that we have but a soldier's life is hard enough. The easiest way you can take it and if he don't find out the difference between living at Mrs. Hoyt's and going a soldiering. I am mistaken however he has but 9 months to serve and I hope he will weather it through.

I suppose you have heard that Dave Mansfield has been reduced to the ranks and transferred to Company D. The reason was that he was thought too much of by the boys and was not sufficiently mean and tyrannical enough to suit

GEORGE NORRIS HAMILTON &
ELI CLARK HAMILTON PROBABLY
APRIL 8, 1864

the colonel whose principle is to have none but the most un-principled and black hearted scoundrels he can find placed in command of us. But there is a day of reckoning coming and woe be unto the hides of some of our officers if the boys ever catch them in Connecticut after the war is over. I tell you it is hard for a free born American to submit to the un-reasonable and degrading restrictions that are put upon us by a set of men whom we despise from the bottom of our heart and whom at home we would consider the scum and offacourings of humanity but I will leave this subject for I cannot find words in the English language sufficiently strong to express my contempt for them. You may think that I ex-aggerate things but if I should tell you one tenth part of the real truth you would consider me either drunk crazy or an infernal …*illegible*… you for it is hard to believe that war will develop such hellish attributes as are displayed by offi-cers having little brief authority. Nate Bornwall, who is in the same tent with me, has just read me a letter that he has been writing his brother in Danbury that gives him his opin-ion good and strong.

Yours,
C. Hamilton

P.S. Write as soon as you get this and give me all the news. I am as well and hearty as ever.

C. Hamilton

IMAGE FROM RETURN ADDRESS ENVELOPE FROM
CLARK HAMILTON TO BROTHER

———————

Notably, this letter was written nine days before Clark left his unit. He was ready to get out, and he did. His official U.S. government military records state that he "deserted" Company A of the Connecticut Eleventh Regiment of Infantry Volunteers in Falmouth, Virginia, on January 19, 1863. [5] His morale at the time was certainly bitter. However, Clark seems to have been quickly captured. His official records next note that on February 4, 1863, he was in Harrisburg, as part of a "detachment of paroled prisoners" on their way to Elmira, New York. Two days later, on February 6, 1863, he signed preliminary enlistment papers in Elmira with Light Battery B of the regular Fifth U.S. Artillery Regiment based in Fort Hamilton, New York Harbor. [6] His official enlistment papers with Battery B were signed in Mar-

5   Official U.S. Military Records of Clark Hamilton, *National Archives and Records Administration.*

6   Ibid.

tinsburg, Virginia on February 29, *1864*. [7] However, those papers established clearly that as of February 6, *1863*, Clark had the status of "enlisted." His reenlistment was to serve the unexpired period of three years. He was described as an "excellent soldier." Moreover, his military file included a later note from the Adjutant General's Office stating that the

> *charge of desertion removed. Enlisted in Co. "B" 5th Artillery at Parole Camp Elmira, N.Y. February 6th, 1863, under G.O. 154 of 1862, to serve out balance of volunteer enlistment.* [8]

Though Clark may have actually deserted the Connecticut Volunteers for a week or two before being captured, he avoided desertion charges by allowing himself to be recruited (either voluntarily or involuntarily) immediately into a regular army unit. General Order 154 saved him.

General Order 154 of October 9, 1862, allowed soldiers from "volunteer" units to immediately transfer to different "regular" Union army units on any date they agreed to with a regular army recruiter, and *without* the permission of the losing volunteer unit. [9] The General Order was very con-

---

7   Army of the United States, Re-enlistment Papers of Clark Hamilton, *Hamilton–Knapp Collection 1742–1924* (Hartford: Connecticut State Library, Archive RG 69:7).

8   Official U.S. Military Records of Clark Hamilton, *National Archives and Records Administration.*

9   Adjutant General's Office, *General Orders Affecting the Volunteer Force 1862* (Washington: Government Printing Office, 1863) pp. 131-132.

troversial, since it permitted the regular army to "recruit," or steal, any volunteers or aspiring deserters it could induce, and the losing state volunteer units were compelled to provide honorable discharges up to the date of transfer. Indeed, Pennsylvania Governor Curtin protested to President Lincoln that the order "was unjust to the people of the States, and calculated to demoralize and destroy the volunteer organizations..." [10] Nevertheless, the Order provided an easy way for Clark Hamilton to escape the tyranny of the Connecticut Volunteers.

Of course, Clark's Connecticut superior officers were certainly displeased, and proved extremely uncooperative in facilitating his transfer. They delayed sending his official papers to his new unit for over a year, thus preventing him from being paid. Battery B's commander sent stinging letters directly to the Adjutant General of the Army complaining about this, all on Clark's behalf on June 5, 1863, on Sep-

---

GENERAL ORDERS, NO. 154
WAR DEPARTMENT, Adjutant General's Office,
Washington, October 9, 1862.

The commanding officer of each regiment, battalion, and battery of the Regular Army in the field, will appoint one or more recruiting officers, who are hereby authorized to enlist, with their own consent, the requisite number of efficient volunteers to fill the ranks of their command to the legal standard.

The enlistments will be made in the usual mode, and for three years, or for the remaining portion of the period of three years which the volunteer has yet to serve, if he so prefer.

The recruiting officers will furnish to the commanding officers of companies to which volunteers whom they may enlist belong, lists of such volunteers, exhibiting the dates of enlistment of each in the Regular Service. All the men upon such lists will be reported as honorably discharged the day previous to the date of their enlistment, on the first subsequent muster roll of their company.

As an inducement to volunteers to enlist in the Regular Army, it will be remembered that promotion to commissions therein is open by law to its meritorious and distinguished non-commissioned officers; and that many have already been promoted.

BY ORDER OF THE SECRETARY OF WAR: L. THOMAS, Adjutant General

10   Abraham Lincoln, *Collected Works of Abraham Lincoln. Volume 5.* (New Brunswick, N.J.: Rutgers University Press, 1953) p. 482.

tember 16, 1863, and again on November 19, 1863. [11] Clark's official file also includes a later statement dated January 14, 1892, confirming yet again that the "charge of desertion against private Hamilton is removed." [12]

Light Battery "B," Fifth U.S. Artillery was first organized in November 1862 at Fort Hamilton, New York Harbor, where it remained until July 1863. After that, it was deployed to Martinsburg, Virginia and to West Virginia. The detailed daily movements of Battery "B" were chronicled, with a register of all Battery members (including Clark Hamilton), by its bugler Richard Wende, and later published. [13]

It seems probable that Clark's transfer to Battery B may have derived from meeting Henry A. Du Pont (of the Du Pont Chemical family) at the battle of Antietam. It appears that Du Pont was providing artillery support to the Connecticut 11th Volunteers as they rushed the Antietam Creek bridge. Du Pont was a West Point friend of Colonel Kingsbury, who was mortally wounded leading the Connecticut Volunteers in the battle. [14] Du Pont went on to assume later command of Battery B.

11   Letters Received by the Office of the Adjutant General, Main Series 1861-1870, *National Archives and Records Administration.*

12   Official U.S. Military Records of Clark Hamilton, *National Archives and Records Administration.*

13   Bugler Richard Wende, *Campaign of Light Battery "B," 5th U.S. Artillery*, Commanded by Captain and Bvt Col. H. A. Du Pont. (Phillipsburg, NJ: E. R. Galligan, 1895)

14   John W. Schildt, *Connecticut at Antietam* (Chewsville, Md: Antietam Publications, 1988) p. 47.

ELI CLARK HAMILTON MARRIES
MARY F. PLOW
APRIL 8, 1864

At least the first half of 1863 Clark spent not far from his Danbury home. After that he was in Virginia. In his last letter below, written one month after his marriage and dated May 10, 1864, Clark talks of finding his way back to Martinsburg after visiting with his brother George Norris Hamilton further north. [15]

---

15   Transcription of original letter from the *Hamilton–Knapp Collection 1742–1924* (Hartford: Connecticut State Library, Archive RG 69:7).

———————

Camp near Strasburg, Virginia
May 10, 1864

Brother Norris,

I received your letter of the 1st and was very glad to hear from you. I also received the papers you sent. Soon after you left us in Jersey City we started, and arrived in Baltimore about 10 o'clock that night. From there, Post went on to Washington to see his brother, and I stopped in Baltimore that night. And the next day being Sunday, I could not get away until 9 o'clock that evening, when I fell in with a squad of soldiers and I came through with them to Harpers Ferry free gratis for nothing and arrived in Martinsburg about 3 o'clock in the morning and found the battery had left three weeks before so I had nothing to do but report to the Provost Marshall's Office which I did about noon and he could give me no information of the whereabouts of the battery but told me told me to remain in Martinsburg until he could find out where it was. But as I was coming out of the office, I met Du Pont and he told me the battery was in Grafton and I could go on with him the next day, which I did. But we only stayed two days. After I got there when we came back to Martinsburg and stopped there a few days, when orders came to march up the valley. And we are now about 18 miles beyond Winchester. We haven't seen nor heard of any rebels in any force.

May 12
Woodstock, Virginia

Since writing the above, we have moved still further up. We are about 12 miles further on. How long we will stay here I don't know. We have had a heavy rain, and it is still raining. And everything is mud and nothing but mud. I saw Lewis Shack today. He belongs to the 1st New York Cavalry but is on duty in the ambulance corps. Post says he don't remember the circumstance you spoke of. He thinks you must be mistaken. Direct your letters the same as you have done. I will write again soon.

Yours,
C. Hamilton

———————

Between Clark's February 1863 reenlistment and his letter of May 10, 1864, he had returned to Connecticut to see his brother and to marry Mary F. Plow on April 8, 1864, in Southeast, New York, 10 miles from Danbury. Mary was newly pregnant at the time. Clark subsequently returned to

ELI CLARK
HAMILTON
APRIL 8, 1864

the battery in Virginia. Since leaving the Connecticut Volunteers in January 1863, there were no indications of any further complaints about the military by Clark.

In Virginia with Battery B, Clark participated in the following battles: New Market (May 15, 1864), Berryville (September 3, 1864), Opequan (September 19, 1864), Fisher's Hill (September 22, 1864), and Cedar Creek (October 19, 1864).

It was in October that things changed for the worse. During the nasty, hard-fought battle of Cedar Creek, Virginia, on October 19, Clark was captured. Confederate forces overran Union positions at 5:30 in the morning during a surprise attack. Many were captured out of their beds. The Rebels immediately captured Clark's artillery battery, including its six three-inch guns. Two of the other batteries, led by Captain Du Pont, escaped, and managed to fire back at the Confederates. Union forces managed to push the Confederates back later in the day. However, Union forces were unable to liberate prisoners. Clark Hamilton was marched off to Confederate prison, though his family was unaware at the time. Du Pont earned the Congressional Medal of Honor for fighting back that day.

Seven months later, on May 29, 1865, the Adjutant General's Office of the War Department informed Norman B. Hamilton that his son, Clark, was dead. [16] Nothing more. On July 26, 1865, Captain Henry A. Dupont of Battery B 5th Artillery Regiment wrote to Clark's father, Norman Hamilton, to explain that Private Clark Hamilton died February 25, 1865, while a prisoner of war during his transfer from Salisbury Prison, North Carolina to Richmond, Virginia, preparatory to being exchanged. His remains were interred at Richmond, Virginia. Clark was described as being very ill during the latter part of his confinement at Salisbury and had to be carried to the cars when he left for Richmond. [17]

It is noteworthy that on February 22, 1865, all Salisbury prisoners not too sick or weak to move, were to leave the prison for a general prisoner exchange. Reportedly the prison water was contaminated and typhoid was rampant. Conditions were deteriorating rapidly. It is reported that

16   Original letter from the *Hamilton–Knapp Collection 1742– 1924* (Hartford: Connecticut State Library, Archive RG 69:7).

17   Original letter from the *Hamilton–Knapp Collection 1742– 1924* (Hartford: Connecticut State Library, Archive RG 69:7).

only 1,800 of 2,800 total survived the 51-mile foot march to Greensboro. The dead were left alongside the road. Clark seems to have been too ill to march, and was sent by cart to Richmond.

More than a year later, another officer (name illegible) from Battery B 5th Artillery Regiment wrote to Norman Hamilton on November 27, 1866, to provide further details. The soldier noted that both he and Clark had been captured at the Battle of Cedar Creek in Virginia on October 19, 1864. They were confined to Libby Prison until October 26, when they were transferred to Salisbury. "Suffering from the effects of starvation and ill treatments in Rebel prisons, he was put on cars for Richmond on February 21, 1865, for the purpose of being paroled but died on the road before reaching Richmond, Virginia." [18] The location of his remains are unknown.

Clark's wife, Mary F. Plow Hamilton, gave birth to a son, Clarkie Hamilton, on November 22, 1864, during the time Clark was in prison. Clark never saw his son. Mary collected a widow's pension from the army for several years. Their son, Clarkie, died on March 14, 1876, at the age of 11 from unknown causes and was buried in Danbury's Pembroke Cemetery. Mary went on and married another war veteran, Frank B. Smith. They were both buried together in Pembroke Cemetery. Clark's brothers, William and Starr, returned to Danbury at the end of the war.

---

18   Original letter from the *Hamilton–Knapp Collection 1742–1924* (Hartford: Connecticut State Library, Archive RG 69:7).

CHAPTER EIGHT

NEW ORLEANS

(1863)

S tarr Hamilton initially avoided the 11th Connecticut Volunteers, and was sent to New Orleans in 1863 with Company G of the 12th Connecticut Infantry Regiment. From there, he writes to brother George Norris Hamilton about the war in the South. [1]

———————

March 9, 1863
Camp St. Charles L.A.

Brother Norris,

I now write you a few lines to know how I am a get-

---

1   Transcription of original letter from the *Hamilton–Knapp Collection 1742–1924* (Hartford: Connecticut State Library, Archive RG 69:7).

ting along down here in the sunny south. I am well and enjoying myself first rate. We are very pleasantly situated here and have first-rate quarters. We have first rate fare and have a rather an easy time of it a guarding the railroad. We have not as yet had any trouble with the rebels but they is a pretty good look for some fighting. Now we have just had news of the capture of one of our gunboats up to Brashear City by the rebels. The captain of the boat was killed and some twenty others ones, and some prisoners taken. They was forty killed out of one company of the 12th C. V. Regiment. They are a expecting an attack up where Company B is. That is up to headquarters. They is several companies there. They got pretty scared last night. They thought the rebels was a coming to attack them. They got all ready for them. Penny Biscuit got scared almost to death. He thought he see a lot of cavalry a coming so he puts off into the swamp and stays there all night. They have been expecting an attack there some time now, and I guess they will be one now. They has just a battery gone up on the cars. They is pretty lively times here now amongst us. If they do come, we are ready for them. It is very warm weather here now. Everything is in full bloom. I wish you could see the gardens here. They are half grown blackberries begin to be ripe. We have some fun in catching alligators. They is lots of them here and everything else. I haven't anything more to write this time. I wish you would write oftener than you do, and write all the news. And if you hear from the Boys, let me know.

From your brother,
Starr Hamilton

Direct your letters the same as you have.

———————

Starr mustered out on August 31, 1863 after fulfilling his enlistment. On February 9, 1864, he enlisted with Company A of the 11th Connecticut Volunteers, where brother William had just reenlisted the month before for another three years. On June 3, 1864, Starr was seriously wounded fighting alongside his brother William at Cold Harbor near Richmond. There are no detailed letters. However, ten months later Starr did write from his hospital bed to his father, Norman B. Hamilton, to reflect on his own spiritual rebirth. [2] He also offered encouragement despite the lack of news about the fate of his brother Clark for over six months. At the time, Starr was wounded, and writes from the hospital about his spiritual rebirth.

———————

Hampton Hospital
Fortress Monroe
April 9th, 1865

———————————

[2]   Transcription of original letter from the *Hamilton–Knapp Collection 1742–1924* (Hartford: Connecticut State Library, Archive RG 69:7).

Dear and ever remembered Father,

It is with pleasure that I now answer your letter, which I received a day or two ago. I was glad to hear from you. I feel sad to think that you cannot hear anything from Clark. I know that it must trouble you a great deal but keep up courage. He may come around yet. I hope that we may all meet again on earth. It would be a joyful time. And if we are not permitted to, may we hope to in that world above where there is no war and all is peace. Dear Father, they has

STARR HAMILTON
DATE ESTIMATED 1883

a change come over me lately. I feel as if I had ought to lead a different life and have so resolved to do. When I look back and see what I have been through, I think that the Lord has been with me. Something seems to say to me go and give yourself to Christ. I have long felt it, and have resisted it until now, and now have resolved to lead a righteous life, may the Lord give me strength. So to, I had a letter from Bill and Hamley the other day. They had not moved then. I suppose now that they are in Richmond by what I see by the papers. I don't think but what they are all right. I am well as usual. My side does not trouble me as much as it did. Things looks now as if the war was about over. By next fall I think that we will be at home and perhaps before. You did not say nothing about the babies. How do they get along. I have no more time to write. Write soon.

From your son,
Starr

———————

Starr was discharged and returned home in 1865. He married Mary Ann Downs of Connecticut, and they had two children, Ella G. Hamilton, who was born around 1867, and Anna A. Hamilton, who, was born around 1869. He worked as a hatter for many years.

William H. Hamilton returned to Danbury after the war and married a lady named Mary J. Her maiden name is unknown.

Elder brother George Norris Hamilton was a farmer in 1860. He reportedly later learned the hatter's trade, which he followed for many years. [3] In 1885 his wife, Mary Eliza Thorpe, died. He and his wife had three children as follows:

Edgar Edward Hamilton was born September 13, 1860. He married Minnie Etta Starr on June 1, 1887, and died October 25, 1919.

Mary A. "Mame" Hamilton was born December 2, 1864. She married George M. Stebbins of Danbury, and died February 8, 1925.

Georgia B. Hamilton was born November 1875. She married John E. Johnston.

Until 1867 the Hamilton family owned large swaths of land around Bear Mountain, Pembroke, and beyond, as indicated in the following 1867 map, courtesy of the Danbury Museum and Historical Society Authority. The disposition of these holdings is unclear, though it would appear that some of the acreage is located where the Margerie Pond reservoir currently exists.

---

3   *Commemorative Biographical Record of Fairfield County, Connecticut*, Part II (Chicago: J.H. Beers & Co., 1899), p. 918.

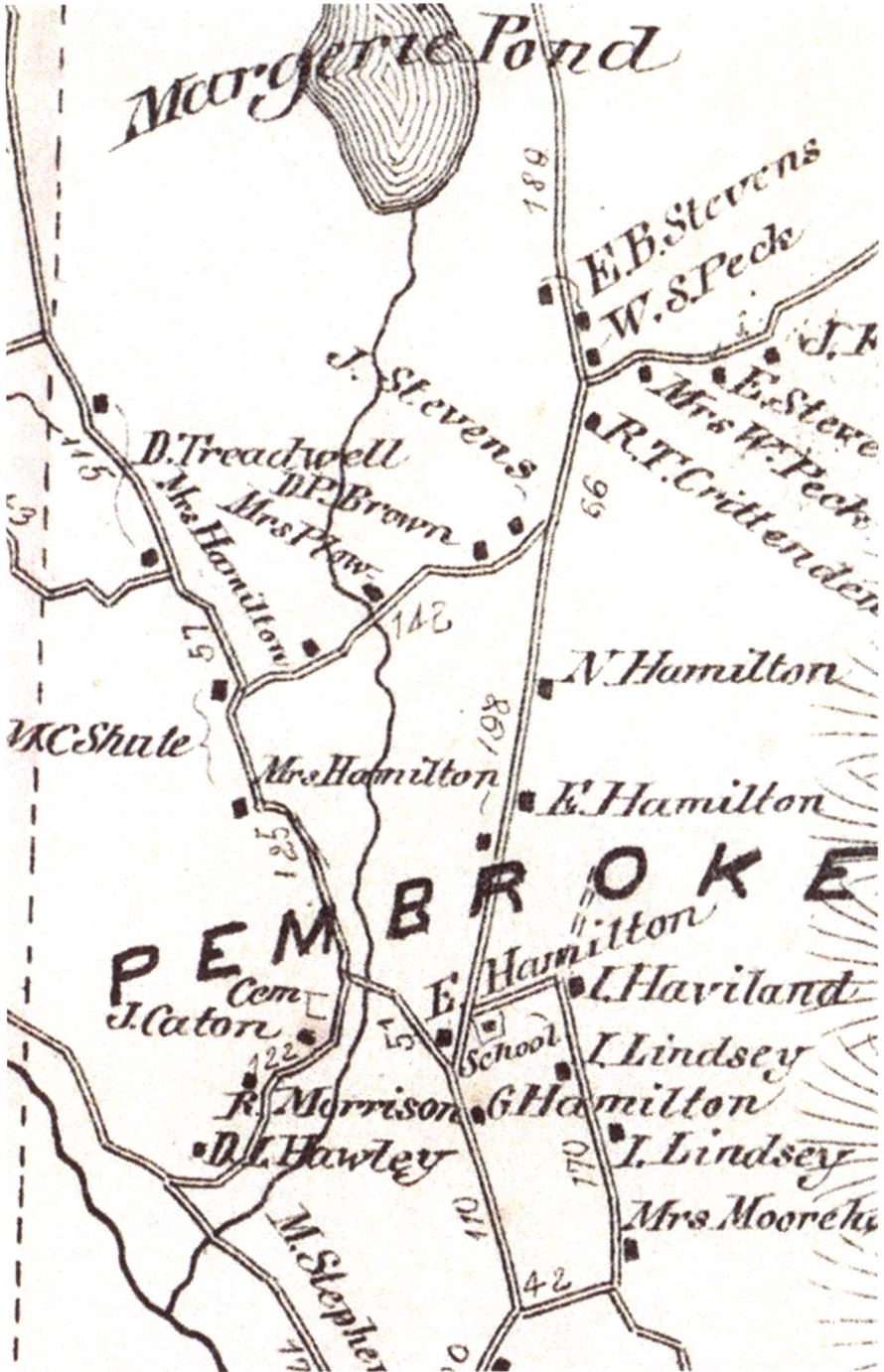

PEMBROKE 1867 SHOWING LAND HELD BY HAMILTONS

CHAPTER NINE

HAMILTON PRESS

(1878)

Edgar Edward Hamilton decided not to continue in farming or hatting. At the age of 18, he founded the Hamilton Press in Danbury in 1878. It was sold 92 years later on October 20, 1970, to F. Jay Tappen. From 1919, the year Edgar died, to 1934 the press was run by his elder son, George Edgar Hamilton.[1]

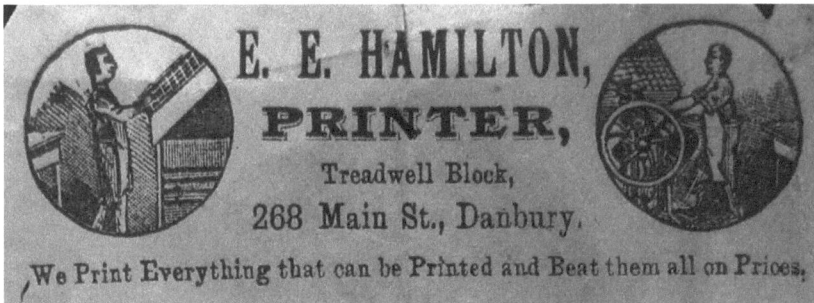

HAMILTON PRESS IMAGE 1885

---

1   Leary, Edward A., John H. Hinton, and Albert E. Hamilton. *60 Years in Danbury 1878-1938* (Danbury: The Hamilton Press, 1938), p. 8.

From 1934 to 1970 Albert Edward Hamilton, son of Edgar, managed the press.

Edgar Hamilton attended local schools. He must have been proud of his school work because his report cards from 1873–1875 were preserved in the family records. He was a very good student, but not outstanding.

Still, he seems to have taken pride in writing well. He crafted the following poem in the autograph book of Danbury resident Flora Downs in 1872. At the time Hamilton composed these impecibly legible, hand-written lines, he was a mere 12 years of age: [2]

Most worthy friend
These lines I send
With my congratulations;
This book I trust
May never rust,
But last for generations.

And all I ask,
('Tis no great task,
So straightway set about it.)
Is this: - Each part
Learn well by heart,
And then stand up and "spout" it.

2   *Autograph Book* of Flora Downs, circa 1872, Courtesy of the Danbury Museum & Historical Society Authority.

May peace and health,
And love and wealth
Be yours in lavish plenty;
And may your grace
Charm many a face,
'Till A.D. 2020.

I hope that you
May live to view
Your great-grandchildrens daughters;
And when at last
This life is past,
All meet across the waters.

Your sincere friend,

E.E. Hamilton

EDGAR EDWARD HAMILTON
CIRCA 1880

Edgar purchased his first printing equipment in 1878, with money he earned picking and selling the apple crop from his father's farm. He set up a printing shop on the grounds of the family homestead on North Main Street, a move that redefined the Hamilton family away from farming and hatting, and into printing. Around 1890 Hamilton moved to larger and more central quarters on the third floor of 268 Main Street directly opposite the railroad station. Here a gasoline engine furnished power for the printing presses, replacing the foot-power treadle.

HAMILTON PRESS 1904
EDGAR HAMILTON SECOND FROM LEFT

When Danbury troops left for duty at the start of the Spanish American War in 1898, enthusiastic Hamilton printers created a near panic when they fired a cannon from the shop's third floor window as a salute. [3], [4]

EDGAR'S KNIGHTS TEMPLAR
SWORD HANDLE

By 1891, Edgar had become a Mason in Danbury. He was a member of the Union Lodge No. 40 Free and Accepted Masons in Danbury, and a member of the Crusader Commandery No. 10, Knights Templars. He was also a Shriner, and a member of the Ecclesiastical Society of the First Congregational Church. [5] Edgar also served as director of the Board of Trade. He was very engaged and apparently well-liked.

Hamilton died in 1919. His elder son, George, born February 21, 1892, took over management of the printing

---

3   *Biography of Edgar Edward Hamilton*, Danbury Museum & Historical Society database, Danbury 2013.

4   Leary, Edward A., John H. Hinton, and Albert E. Hamilton. *60 Years in Danbury 1878–1938* (Danbury: The Hamilton Press, 1938), pp. 1–8.

5   *Danbury Evening News*, Obituaries section, October 27, 1919.

business. Under his guidance the business grew, and in 1927 it was moved to its own building on Post Office Street. In 1934, the founder's younger son, Albert, took over from his brother. He sold the business in 1970.

———

MINNIE ETTA STARR
CIRCA 1890

The *Danbury News-Times* reported in an obituary on January 25, 1952, that Minnie Etta Starr, Edgar's wife, died the previous night. She was a descendant of one of Danbury's earliest settlers, Comfort Starr, who was credited with founding Danbury's first school. In his will, Comfort Starr had left 800 pounds "lawful money for the support of a school in the center of the town, to be under the direction of the civ-il authority and selectmen; the instruction to be capable of teaching reading, writing and arithmetic, Latin and Greek languages, &c. During the War of Revolution this fund de-preciated to the sum of 488 pounds, 12s. 9d. By Act of the Conn. Legislature, passed May session, 1798, this school was converted into a school of higher order." [6]

Comfort Starr's great-great-grandfather, also named Dr. Comfort Starr, was an early immigrant to Boston. That Dr. Comfort Starr had brought his family from Kent, En-gland, to New Towne (now Cambridge), where he reestab-lished his surgery practice in 1635. According to family history, Dr. Starr's house became the home of Nathaniel Ea-ton and served in 1639 as the site where Harvard College instruction began. The Reverend Comfort Starr, one of Dr. Comfort Starr's nine children, was the first family member to graduate from the College (in 1647), and is one of five Fellows named in the Harvard College Charter of 1650, the document that officially incorporated the school. [7]

A daughter of the late Harry Starr and Eliza (Hodges) Starr, Minnie Etta Starr Hamilton was born in Danbury on January 19, 1862, and spent her lifetime as a resident of the city. She was one of the oldest members of the First Con-gregational church. She remained secretary at the Hamilton

6   Burgis Pratt Starr, *A History of the Starr Family* (Hartford, CT: Case, Lockwood & Brainard Company, 1879), p. 270.

7   *Harvard University Gazette*, date unknown as quoted at www. http://home.everestkc.net/4dbteague/HarvardandtheStarrFam-ily.html <3 October 2015>

Press until the time of her death. She resided at 9 North Street but spent the last 28 months of her life at Twin Pines Convalescent home in Northville. She died at age 90. [8]

———————

Edgar and Minnie had five children as follows, only two of whom survived to adulthood:

Edgar E. Hamilton was born December 19, 1888, and was stillborn.

Paul Hamilton was born November 1895 and died January 26, 1896.

Mildred S. Hamilton was born February 1890 and died March 1, 1900.

George Edgar "Teddy" Hamilton was born February 21, 1892. He married Marion Norton Allen of Hartford. After her early death, he later married Vera Louise Hale of Tennessee. He died February 14, 1964, in Memphis, Tennessee.

Albert Edward Hamilton was born September 30, 1902. He married Ellen Marie Walberg, and died July 26, 1974, in Danbury. They had two sons, Edward R. Hamilton

———————

8   *The Danbury News–Times*, Obituaries section, January 25, 1952.

and William Albert Hamilton, who reside in Connecticut and are engaged in the book business.

CHAPTER TEN

OUT OF DANBURY

G eorge E. "Teddy" Hamilton graduated from Yale University in the Class of 1914. His transcripts indicate he was a B student.   According to the *Yale History of the Class of Nineteen Fourteen*, Teddy was known as "Hammy" in college. [1] He contributed to the *Yale News*, and was chairman of the *Courant*. He was a member of Beta Theta Pi. He expected to enter journalism. On June 5, 1917, he registered for the WWI draft in Hartford, describing himself at the time as an

GEORGE EDGAR
HAMILTON 1914

---

1   George Washington Patterson, IV, editor, *History of the Class of Nineteen Hundred and Fourteen Yale College*, Volume One (New Haven: Yale University Press, 1914), p. 185.

editor of the *Hartford Times* newspaper. On June 22, 1918, he was inducted into the army and sent to Camp Gordon, Georgia. He received an honorable discharge on December 7, 1918. He then took over the Hamilton Printing business when his father died on October 25, 1919. He married Marion Norton Allen of Hartford sometime thereafter, and they had one son, George Newton Hamilton on November 3, 1925.

Around 1934, Teddy and Marion moved to Upper Darby, Pennsylvania, where Teddy worked as an editor for the *Philadelphia Inquirer*. His brother, Albert Edward Hamilton, took over the Danbury Hamilton Printing business at his departure. Albert ran the printing business, until he sold it in October 1970 upon his retirement. Albert and his wife Ellen remained in Danbury their entire lives. They had two

ALBERT EDWARD HAMILTON
1928

sons, Edward R. Hamilton and William Albert Hamilton. Albert was a well-respected civic leader in Danbury. He reportedly was devoted to history, contributed articles to local newspapers, and served on several town planning boards. He began working in his father's print shop in 1918, and took over the company in 1934. He was a member of the Union Lodge and Eureka Chapter of Masons. He was very active in the Lions Club. His children and grandchildren remained involved in the book business in Connecticut, not far from Danbury. They were described in a 1996 history of Danbury's First Congregational Church as living descendants of the original Danbury church families going back over 200 years. [2]

Marion Norton Allen, Teddy's wife, was descended from lengthy and patriotic lineage dating back to renowned Deacon George Graves, who was born in Braintree, England, in 1605. He was an original proprietor before 1640 in Hartford, Connecticut. His home lot was on the highway now known as Elm Street, near the Little River. He was a weaver. He died September 5, 1673.

Another predecessor of Marion's was Lieutenant Nathaniel Stevens, Esquire, who was born about 1661. He

2   ***300th Anniversary, The First Congregational Church, 1696-1996*** (Danbury: First Congregational Church, May 19, 1996), p. 86.

served in the military during Queen Anne's War. In 1705 he was commissioned a Lieutenant. He died October 22, 1709.

A Captain Nathaniel Stevens, Esquire, was also a predecessor of Marion. In 1740 he was commissioned lieutenant, and then in 1741 he was commissioned captain of the 6th Company in the 7th Regiment. He died March 9, 1747.

Marion also was descended from Timothy Munger, who was born September 5, 1735, in Guilford, Connecticut.[3] Munger served first in the military during the French and Indian War. He enlisted on May 30, 1758, as a private in the 5th Company, 1st Regiment and was discharged on December 13, 1758. He reenlisted in related units twice more and in 1771 the Connecticut Assembly "Do establish Timothy Monger to be Ensign in the 14th company or train-band of the seventh regiment in this Colony." [4] He later served in the military during the American Revolution. In June 1776 he was chosen lieutenant of the 14th Company, in Colonel Andrew Ward's 7th Connecticut Militia Regiment. He then became a captain in 1779.

Munger is sometimes credited with having had three wives, however it is unclear whether he ever married two of them.

Marion Norton Allen Hamilton was an only child.

3　　　　Marion A. Hamilton, *Daughters of the American Revolution*, Membership 245435, May 14, 1928.

4　　　　J.B. Munger, *The Munger Book 1639–1914* (Tuttle, Morehouse & Taylor Company, 1915), p. 19.

Her parents were Charles Anthony Allen and Leila May Norton.[5] She succumbed to lung cancer on February 24, 1944, at the age of 50, leaving Teddy with their only child, George Newton Hamilton, who was 19 at the time. She was buried in the Hamilton family plot in Danbury's Wooster Cemetery.

GEORGE NEWTON HAMILTON
1944

Several years later, Teddy married Vera Louise Hale, known as Louise, from Union City, Tennessee. They apparently met in Philadelphia while Teddy was working for the *Philadelphia Inquirer* as an editor. Louise had previously been married to Joseph F. Baxter from Tennessee. However,

5   J.B. Munger, *The Munger Book 1639–1914* (Tuttle, Morehouse & Taylor Company, 1915), p. 155.

he had died in March 1944, coincidentally, one month after Marion died.

On April 23, 1954, Teddy and Louise bought a (at the time) country house at 2606 Pickertown Road, Warrington Township (Doylestown), Pennsylvania. She enjoyed yard-work; she planted 10 pine trees near the house as a gift to her then-only grandson, whom she called Bud. She became seriously ill around 1958, but kept high spirts throughout. On July 14, 1959, Louise died at the age of 52 from lung cancer. She was cremated, and her urn rests alongside that of her first husband, Joseph Baxter, in the upstairs office building of Chelten Hills Cemetery in Philadelphia.

Teddy suffered for the rest of his life from terrible depression and bouts of alcoholism. His doctor wrote about him in a 1963 letter, noting that:

> *This gentleman has had a rather interesting, but also very sad history. He has had the unusual tragedy of losing not one, but two beloved wives by cancer of the lung. These two experiences of course, would be enough to depress any person. However, George has had several other experiences in his life which have been disillusioning and which have caused him to have great internal conflict and have contributed to a very severe depression which he has been suffering since the*

death of his second wife....I was completely unable to get him involved in any activites here in Doylestown.[6]

As a child, the author met him several times in Doylestown. From the eyes of an eight-year-old, he seemed to have had little sense of humor, and demanded strict discipline and hard schoolwork. He enjoyed a strong drink at the local country club in the afternoon. He was always interested in U.S. history, though he was quite reticent to speak.

After the death of his second wife, Teddy sold the house in February 1960, and in October 1963 moved to Memphis, where he spent his remaining months with Louise's sister Gladys. He died there on February 14, 1964, of cerebral arteriorsclerosis. He was buried with his first wife, Marion, in Wooster Cemetery in Danbury.

George Newton Hamilton, sole child of Teddy and Marion, served in WWII before marrying Mildred Helen Hitchens in Philadelphia in June 1948. George was a student at Temple at the time. Mildred worked at Penn Mutual Life Insurance Company, and later as a secretary for the Schenley Whiskey Company. They had one son, George A. Hamilton.

In 1954 George Newton Hamilton unexpectedly abandoned Mildred and his infant son. He moved to San Diego, California, in the company of Thelma Mae Ziedler Janka, whom he subsequently married in Las Vegas. George

---

6   Letter from A. Thomas Ritchie, MD to George Edgar Hamilton, for use on introduction to new physician. October 16, 1963. From author's collection.

Newton Hamilton ran a large car dealership in California for many years. He and Thelma had two children, Lynne and Gregg, in California. George Newton Hamilton died in San Diego on March 13, 1999.

Mildred subsequently divorced George Hamilton and married Arthur Allen Glass. They resided in Glassboro, New Jersey; Richardson, Texas; Cape May, New Jersey; and Deptford, New Jersey. Arthur Glass worked for Mobil Oil Company as an accountant for 41 years. He was also elected to serve on the Glassboro town council for a number of years during the 1960s. He was a dedicated member of the Democratic Party. He died January 9, 1996, and Mildred died October 23, 2000. Their remains are interred in Eglington Cemetery.

On August 28, 1951, the Town of Danbury established and named a street on Bear Mountain as Hamilton Drive.[7] The street is in the area where the Hamiltons of 1867 owned a substantial amount of land. By early in the new millenium, the original Hamilton line of Danbury had moved on beyond a city that had changed markedly.

Or perhaps not? On October 13, 2015, the author was driving around Marjorie Reservoir, imagining the old land routes before modern times. A small roadside cemetery came into view in New Fairfield. Judging from the thin, leaning tombstones, it was ancient. Why not take a look? Passing the entry gate and strolling to the middle, the author

---

7   See Town of Danbury, *Land Records Book Number 257* (Danbury Clerk's Office: Danbury, 1951) p. 167.

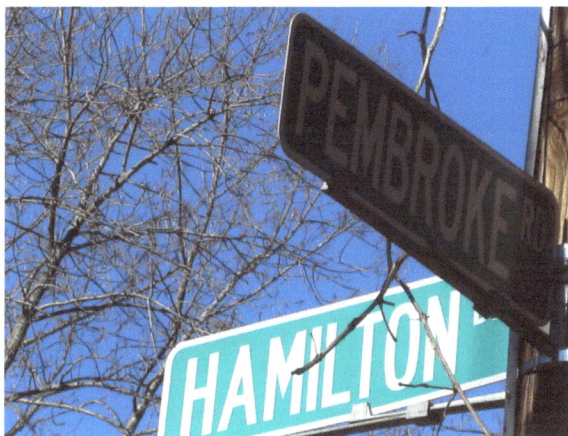

HAMILTON DRIVE, PEMBROKE,
DANBURY 2013

selected just one single gravestone to examine out of curiosity. Pause. It turned out to be the grave of young Hannah
Hamilton Brush, who died in 1774 at the young age of 20
after only one year of marriage. She was immediately recog-
nizable from the inscription, though the stone did not bear
her Hamilton maiden name.

This was the oldest now-discovered grave of the early
Hamilton era. Her grandfather, Silas, bequeathed in 1790
part of his substantial land holdings to her husband, Eliphalet Brush, who was a captain in the Revolutionary War. [8]
There are no other Hamiltons apparent in the cemetery, but
the cemetery sits on Brush Hill road in New Fairfield. Ser-
endipity? The road was indeed named after Eliphalet's father,
Thomas Brush, another captain in the Revolutionary War.

---

8   From the *1785 Will of Silas Hamilton*, Probated in Danbury,
Connecticut on November 13, 1790.

DIARY OF
GEORGE N. HAMILTON, 1856

CONNECTICUT STATE ARCHIVES
HAMILTON KNAPP COLLECTION, RG 69:07

Transcribed by Kristen N. Keegan
November 2013

(Omitted: Marriage & death notices pasted into front cover.)

PAGE 1

Journal 1856

March 31 1856

Left home for the West at the depot met M E T & C A T who came to see me start waited a short time for the cars to leave the time came at last and I took lave leave of my friends with feelings that can be better imagined than described had sufficient control over my feelings however to master

PAGE 2

them at last I then felt better I saw a countenance at the depot as the train left I shall always remember the sight[ing] of it came very near making a child of me I arrived in New York at 11 oclock went over to Brooklyn saw several Danbury folks returned to the city & then crossed over to Jersey City saw N [Turrel] & stopped with him over night left New York at 8 oclock

PAGE 3

the next morning for Monticello & arrived there at 7 oclock in the Evening & found all the friends well as usual stayed there and spent the week left Monday Morning for the West took the cars at Middletown at [noon] & arrived at Owego [sic] about 9 oclock in the Evening took supper & retired early in order to take the 3 oclock express the next morning rose at 12 midnight to be in season for

PAGE 4

the Train the Train was behind time [waited] untill [sic] 4 oclock when I left fond [sic] the cars all full arrived at Hor[ ]ville at 8 AM being 1½ hours behind time we finally got under way again for Buffalo and after being detained reached Buffalo at 2 PM instead of 11 AM as we should have done lost the connection & consequently had to remain there over night on the Buffalo road we ran through

PAGE 5

Banks of Snow higher than the top of the cars saw some fine country in the line of the Erie Road the fines [sic] I ever Saw left Buffalo the next morning on the [9] AM train for Dunkirk arrived there at 9 oclock on the cars came across a young fellow from Hartford Ct & we struck up an acquaintance immediately & agreed to keep each other company had to Stop at Dunkirk to get my Trunk checked my friend had to do

PAGE 6

the same or expected to but his Baggage had not arrived so I waited for the next train which was due at noon the Lightning Express but my friends trunk did not come & I had to part with him much to my regret saw a great many beautiful sights in the way arrived at Cleveland at 7 oclock being behind time again left there with 12 long cars filled to overflowing continued to lose

PAGE 7

time all the way to Toledo reached there at 2 oclock in the morning instead of 11 at night as we should have done on the way the Engine got detached from the train & ran about 5 miles before the Engineer saw the he was without the train found all the Hotels full I had for a bed two [bar room] chairs & a carpet bag for a Pillow slept two hours pretty comfortably left the next morning at 7 am

PAGE 8

for Chicago I think Toledo is the vilest place I ever saw & the most villainous looking set of men anyone could wish to see I made up my mind it was the first & & last time I should step there I was glad when the time came for the cars to start such a rush for seats I never saw before we had a train of 17 cars all full had to run slow & did not reach Chicago untill [sic] 9 in the Evening should have been in by 6 am

PAGE 9

Put up at the Merchants Hotel in company with a couple of young fellows from the East whose acquaintance I made they were bond [sic] to Minnesota after supper took a walk and returned early sleep a little something I had not done in some time rose eat breakfast & set out to find the Danbury people saw Mr Benedict Mr Malloy [Keeler] & Bill Putnam all of them were supprised [sic] to see me

PAGE 10

Called to see Mrs Thorp who did not know what to say she was so supprised [sic] she appeared glad to see me stayed about 2 hours recived [sic] an invitation to stay to stay to dinner but declined ate my dinner at the Hotel then went to the Depot of the Mich Central RR to see M H T] found him shook him by the hand & had quite a talk with him about matters & things had an invitation

PAGE 11

to take tea with him accepted had a good time stayed all Night Saturday Evening went to the Theater with him saw some good plays & arrived here in good Season

Sunday Apr 13

arose at 7 went out for a walk returned took Breakfast then took another walk a fine day to be out in the Evening attended church heard a good Sermon

PAGE 12

Apr 14

a stormy morning the rain pours down in torrents with a clap of thunder occasionly [sic] for variety took a walk around the city in the afternoon Apr 15 I arose & eat Breakfast & commenced preparations to go out to Ottawa to see G H Norris & Family left Chicago & after a ride of 3 hours found myself in Ottawa found Mr Norris & introduced myself to him and was cordially received

PAGE 13

eat dinner & then went out to see the city which I found to be a very pretty place it is the best farming country I ever saw had a talk with him about business matters and he advised me to go to Minnesota & take up a piece of Land he told me it was the best thing I could do I think it would not suit me

& shall try & see what I can do in Chicago before I go farther West

PAGE 14

Apr 16

a warm pleasant day busied myself with walking & riding about the city got some letters of introduction to men in Chicago

Apr 17

left Ottawa for Chicago stoped [sic] at Jolliet saw [R Keeler] took dinner with him left at 4 oclock for Chicago arrived at 6 called at the P Office & got two letters from Home which did me a vast amount of good

PAGE 15

Apr 18 + 19

weather cool walked about to see what was the prospect for business think I shall succeed after I get a little more acquaint-ed with the People Apr 20 Sunday walked about the city saw a great many pretty Ladies they [dress out] very Strong

Apr 21 22

Walking about for [business] had an introduction to several R R men who have promised to give

PAGE 16

me a chance by & by

May 8

have got tired of looking after a situation here & think the Prospect not very flattering saw H H Morris to day & have made an arrangement with him to assist him this summer & go in Monday

May 10

am at my new place of business not much to do think I shall have an easy turn this Summer

PAGE 17

I have neglected my Journall [sic] Mr Morris has taken a P[asture?] & has no further use for me I think it is to [sic] bad but it cant [sic] be helped

May 27

I met G H Norris to day & was glad to see him he has been talking Minnesota to me & I have concluded to go shall leave before long

PAGE 18

May

another blank I have met all of Danbury in the past week
Mr E T Hoyt R M[arsh?] Orrin Benedict L [Keeler] Rev Mr
Grimm[ ] and a lot of others

June 9

one more Jump I hope I shall be able to keep my journal a
little better than I have heretofore left Chicago this morning
for Rockford found

PAGE 19

all of the people stayed all night with Mr Harris I like the
place very much it seems pleasant to get out of Chicago

June 10

went up to see Uncle Daniel Barnums folk found them all
well and glad to see me it is a fine country around here spent
the day & returned at Night on our way home saw a field
with 3 hundred acres in it it was a

PAGE 20

splendid sight

June 11

Went out to see E Ham[ilton] & spent the afternoon find ET

the same as usual he lives a little to [sic] much in the Hermit order to suit me in the Evening went home with Harris Barn[um] & stayed all Night & came in town the next morning

June 12

came to town to see the folks called to see Mr Norman &

PAGE 21

spent the day stopped with Mr Harris all Night expect to leave on Saturday for the River I have company Mr Price & Benedict they left this morning I am to meet them in Dunleith Saturday

June 13

Am in Rockford yet but expect to leave to morrow at 1 oclock Mr Price has gone to day saw A Barnum yesterday & his mother & the Judge all were

PAGE 22

were well & looked as natural as ever

June 14

Called in the forenoon to see Mr E Galgorzos people found them all well was well pleased with the Girls had a good visit stayed to dinner & took the cars at 1 oclock for Dunleith ar-

rived there at 7 oclock was met at the Depot by Mr Price Mr
Benedict arrived soon saw the Mississippi for the first time
did not look as large

PAGE 23

as I expected took Passage on board the Steam Packet Tish-
erming Tishomingo for Winona have a fine man for a Captain like him first rate had a good Supper & retired early but
did not get much sleep fare 125 lower than I expected ($3 00

June 15

rose early a foggy morning it soon cleared away and we have
a warm pleasant day eat breakfast then

PAGE 24

took a seat on deck to see the country saw a magnificcent
[sic] sight all day it is pleasant to steam it up the river I am in
good spirits have heard since I came on board that Minnesota was a Beautiful country I like our Captain he is so sociable
and pleasant I think he is a fine fellow he told me if I ever
rode with anyone else going up or down the

PAGE 25

river he would throw me in to the Drink had a Splendid dinner reached La Crosse at 2 PM tried to find Mr Stevens of
Danbury but did not succeed passed an Indian encampment
on the way & saw the Red men looking at us with conster-

nation reached Winona at 6 oclock a small place but prettily located a fine place for a Town or city to grow up stopped at the Winona House

PAGE 26

took tea wrote home and then took a stroll about the place like it very much expect to go into the country on the morrow

June 16

Left Winona for the country Monday morning at 9 oclock taking a Western course traveled through a rough broken country untill [sic] noon & stopped at a settlement for dinner found 4 houses in the place or rather cabins it looked a little Westernfied the name

PAGE 27

of the place was [Stockton] left after dinner for St Charles 20 miles distant and arrived there at 5 oclock rode through a fine country but it was thinly Settled found 10 cabins in St Charles I begin to think I am out West eat supper and retired early slept in a bed room with about 20 persons apiece [sic] of cloth hung up served as a partition for the Ladies room had a great amount of Sport a regular Backwoods time a dark rainy Night

PAGE 28

June 17

rose a [sic] 6 o'clock eat Breakfast and left soon after for Rochester 23 miles distant arrived there about noon east dinner & took a look at the place find it to be a beautiful place for a Town Site several good frame buildings in the place but the principal part of the houses were Log Cabins Spent the afternoon & Night & made a great many enquirys [sic] about making claims find them taken up for miles

PAGE 29

around I never saw such a rush for land as there is here saw about 30 Waggons [sic] all bound to the West I begin to get a little down hearted about the prospects saw a man & Hired out to him to work on a farm for 19 dollars per month think I shall work a while & then if the prospect does not brighten shall leave for Illinois & try there

PAGE 30

June 18

Left Rochester on a prospecting tour to look up and make a claim started on foot for a place 7 miles North East of Rochester on the way saw a deer go bounding acost [sic] the Prairie the first one I ever saw walked through the woods & [prares] untill [sic] noon came to a Hut & took dinner after dinner lef [sic] in company with some others for

PAGE 31

a [prarie] two miles north saw some that was very nice & succeeded in making some claims returned at dark tired almost out think I was never so tired in my life begin to think the Backwoods is not the place for me

June 19

rose and eat Breakfast could hardly walk from the efforts of yesterdays [sic] work went to work for the man I hired out to had to give

PAGE 32

it up untill [sic] the next day wrote a letter home one to M H T Chicago one to G H Norris Ottawa one to M E T a warm day hired out on a farm to work for Mr Lowry for 6 weeks think I shall like the place very well have left the other man didnt [sic] like him at all at all [sic] took dinner with my my [sic] new man & are to stay with him to night & go to work

PAGE 33

to morrow hope I shall be suited I begin to brighten up a little as my money was [running] low think I shall be somebody yet hope so

June 20

commenced work to day at farming it dint [sic] go good & I think it will be of short duration I have taken it easey [sic] and intend to [dont] think I shall not kill myself with [labor] labor this summer

PAGE 34

June 21

Still hard at work it goes hard though & I think Jordan is a hard road to travel think of home and almost wish I was there

June 22

Sunday has come at last and I am glad to See it wrote to mother to day and M E T G P Smith & cousin A Barnum it has been a long & to me rather lonesome day live in hopes of seeing better days before long

PAGE 35

June 29

Have skipped one week have been working at this & that all the week did not amount to much anyway but it served to pass away the time and that is all I care for begin to like the country a little better than I did a week ago think there will be a chance this fall for me to do something a little easeyer [sic] & better than

PAGE 36

farming shall try hard & see what I can find to amuse myself about this Winter if I dont [sic] find anything here I shall try Winona and so work down the river it is a [fri]day attended church this forenoon for the first time in my life in a Log Scool [sic] House had a regular Western Preacher saw two pretty girls the only ones I have seen since I have been in the place

PAGE 37

wrote two letters today one to B A H & one to M E I I expect a letter to night from Chicago from M A T went to the Post Office bud did not get a letter

June 30

very pleasant weather nothing of importance to note down

July 1st

today is the first of July three months to day since I left home it does not seem but a short time

PAGE 38

July 2d

Still at work but live in hope I shall find some other business one of these days that will suit me better than working on a [Planta]

July 3d

have not done much to day am taking things very cool warm weather

July 4

a pleasant day to day am not at work I little thought one year to day

PAGE 39

I should be here in Minnesota to day but such is life ever changing and changeful attended a Kansas meeting[1] heard some specimens of Western eloquence which called to mind speeches I had seen in Papers illustrative of the Oraters [sic] of the West

July 5

a warm day dont [sic] feel like work to day am heartily tired

PAGE 40

and sick of farming shall find something else to do before long or else do nothing for to work a farmer I cant [sic] nor wont [sic] have thought of home to day & the friends in Dan-

---

1   Presumably a meeting about the ongoing conflict in Kansas over whether its residents would vote to make it a slave state or a free state; partisans on both sides were widely recruited in other states and territories.

bury would like to see them a short time went to the Post Office at night expected to get a letter but was disappointed

July 6

a warm day

PAGE 41

attended church in the forenoon in the afternoon read & slept & passed the remainder of the day saw a Mr Bennet talk of going to work for him in a Brick yard think I shall go & quit farming for the present

July 7

a warm day work goes hard shall try something else before long

July 8

another hot day a

PAGE 42

hard matter to work alone here thought of home and all the friends Hired out to work at making Brick and shall quit farming before long went to the Post Office in the Evening and got a letter from G A Norris expected to hear from [home] but was disappointed

July 8

a hot day have got so I hate

PAGE 43

farming like Poison & shall [wind?] up this work anyway

July 10

went to the Post Office to night & received 3 letters one from M A Thorp & one M E T one from R A H was very glad to hear from home once more

July 11

wrote 3 letters one to B A H one to M E T and one to M H I Chicago

PAGE 44

July 12

nothing of importance to note

July 13

Sunday again a warm day passed the day very pleasantly

July 14

went to the Post Office in the Evening received a letter from M E T & a note from C A T was very much pleased to hear from them

July 15

a very warm day

PAGE 45

July 16

same as yesterday Hot Hotter Hottest

July 17

Nothing

July 18

wrote 3 letters East one to mother one to C A T one to M E T very warm weather July 19 sco[r]ching Hot day have taken things easy to day went to the Post Office in the evening expecting to get a letter but the mail did not come

PAGE 46

July 20 Sunday

Rose in the morning with a violent Headacke [sic] and an awful sore throat the effects of going into the water when I was warm felt miserable and thought of Home and the friends who are far far away a feeling of lonsomeness [sic] came on me and I attended church in the forenoon after church was out saw a company of Indians dressed out in their Indian costume with

PAGE 47

their Ponies & luggage there was 15 or 20 in all including Men Women & children went to the Post Office in the Evening got three letters from the East one from M E T one from Brother Clark and one from G P Smith three very interesting epistles

July 21

a very warm day feel most sick

July 21

home sick with my cold I never had such a Hard cold in my

PAGE 48

life it makes me feel very Bad

July 22

My cold is no better I am about used up wrote a letter to G P Smith Dreadful Hot weather

July 23

Hot Hoter [sic] Hotest [sic] Hotentot Hotentotest Hotento-tismo Hotentoten Ho[ ] my cold is a little better & I begin to feel a little more like myself wrote

PAGE 49

two letters home one to Bro Clark & one to M E T

July 24

Nothing Special I find it to be rather hard work to keep a Journal in such a place as this

July 25

very warm weather yet and like to be a fine growing time July 26 another week is passed & gone went to the Post Office in the Evening expecting to get a letter from home but did not think I

PAGE 50

shall get one on Monday Evening

July 27

went out in the Prairie about 10 miles to day to get a Girl but could not get Her a warm day saw a country that looked Westernfied a good deal I thought July 28 went to the Post office in the Evening got 3 Letters one from B A H one M E T & one from A A Stevens La Crosse

July 29

a warm day am

PAGE 51

doing but very little work about these days July 30
wrote two letters to the East have been Hawling [sic] Hay

July 31

tinkering around as usual I have strong thoughts of leaving my place & go where I can get more wages I have had 5 men speak to have me come & help them will pay 30 per

PAGE 52

month 10 dollars more than I get a present I shall leave here as soon as I can

Aug 1

four months away from home it dont [sic] seem to me as though I had been away only so many weeks it is astonishing how the time runs away

Aug 2

a cool [pleasant] day left to day and am going to a new

PAGE 53

place to work where I can get more wages settled up had 26 dollars coming which was paid me

Aug 3

like my new home first rate it seems like home & I am as contented as a man can be

Aug 4

have been to work to day Haying it [   ] it will

Aug 5

still at work

Aug 6

Same as yesterday am glad I have

PAGE 54

got such a good place there is 10 of us here all yong [sic] fellows

Aug 7

worked all day in the evening went to the Post Office got three Letters one from B A H one from Clark one M E T

Aug 8

Still at work

Aug 9

worked half a day it rained in the afternoon so we could not do any

PAGE 55

Aug 10

wrote three letters home one to M E Y one to Clark & B A H

Aug 11

went to the P Office in the Evening got one letter from the East was disappointed as I expected more

Aug 12

a very pleasant day

Aug 13

the same as yesterday think some of leaving here & going farther into the Territory

PAGE 56

14

warm & Pleasant have made an arrangement to go 50 miles North of here to stay a while think I shall go

Aug 15

a very hot day

Aug 16

Have got through Haying for the present & shall go at something else

Aug 17

wrote a letter to

PAGE 57

M E T one to myself

Aug 18

Have been chopping to day went to the P Office in the Evening got one letter

Aug 19

worked but half a day to day it is to [sic] hard work for me to chop wood

Aug 20

Have been at work digging a mill race like it better than cutting wood

Aug 21

worked but half

PAGE 58

a day felt unwell in the afternoon

Aug 22

Rained in the morning so I could not do anything to day

Aug 23

went out a [work] hunting to day but did not find anything that suited me

Aug 24

a pleasant day had a frost last Night

PAGE 59

Aug 25

commenced work for Rev Mr Reynolds to day at 7 dollars per week have been chopping to day I am 1 ½ miles from [town]

Aug 26

Same as yesterday 13 of us living in a little Log Hut about as large as a snuff Box [we] [all/are] as [thick] as three in a bed, it is western life in earnest I think

PAGE 60

Aug 27

Same as yesterday

Aug 28

Do Do[2]

Aug 29

I have made an arrangement with the Elder to Pre Empt a quarter Section for him for [$1,00] [dols] shall commence as soon as I can

---

2   This is short for "Ditto Ditto," and of course "ditto" means "the same again."

Aug [20/30]

have been at work all day cutting wood

Aug [29]

worked ½ a day

PAGE 61

Aug [28/30]

Have been burning Lime all day find it hot work

Aug 31 Sunday

Fried at the Lime Kiln in the afternoon & Saturday Evening from 12 oclock untill morning

Sep 1

Still a fireman

Sep 2

Do Do

Sep 3

Same as heretofore

PAGE 62

Sept 4

Have been drawing Logs on my Claim preparatory to puting [sic] up a Hut

Sep 5

Have been at work to day quarring [sic] stone to turn another Kiln wrote a letter to mother to day

Sept 6

a rainy morning got a letter from B A H wrote one in afternoon went to

PAGE 63

my claim came up a shower and I got wet through

Sept 7

a pleasant day full mort sick lay a bed all day almost wrote a letter to M E T

Sept 8

arose feeling mort sick have the [Reumatism] beside came to town to my old Home and spent the day

Sep 9

some stiff with

PAGE 64

the Reumatism [sic] felt sick all day took some Pills am going to bed & hope to feel better in the morning

Sept 10

Feel a little better to day a good deal more like myself

Sept 11

went up to my claim & put up my cabin to day

Sept 12

been at work today

PAGE 65

getting cut stone

Sept 13
at work getting cut stone

Sept 14

came to town last Evening to my old home a warm day to

day wrote a letter to M E T and went to church all day

Sept 15

arose at 7 feeling quite unwell did not work any Sept 16 felt about sick all day have the Reumatism [sic]

PAGE 66

so that I cant [sic] stir Had a hard time last night am sick to day lay abed all day hope to be better tomorrow

Sept 17

Felt much better to day think of going to Winona tomorrow after a Load of Goods for J R Cook a Merchant of this place

Sept 18

left Rochester this morning and at 7 this Evening found my-self in Winona

PAGE 67

Sept 19

Arose at 6 this morning was very much supprised [sic] at the growth of this Place since I last saw it saw T D Rogers here this morning was pleased to see him and he appeared to be very much Pleased to see me gave some good advise [sic] and encouragement and we Parted to meet again soon I hope left Winona at 9 for Home drove all day

PAGE 68

and stopped for the Night at a place called Utica a great place to [sic] one House in Eight was all that comprised the village a Western Town in earnest

Sept 21

Went to church half a day wrote three Letters Home one to M E T one to B A H and one to
Mother

Sept 22

Have done nothing to day but am going to work to morrow for Mr Whiting for a Month

PAGE 69

Sept 23

Have been fixing up the School House to day went to the Post Office in the Evening got two Letters from the East one from M E T and one from B A H

Sept 24

Still at work at the old Log School House

Sept 25

the same as yesterday Have at last got it finished all right and tight

PAGE 70

Sept 26

Have been Picking corn to day all day a Pleasant day

Sept 27

Have been at a [bunch?] of things to day attended a Mass Meeting in the afternoon quite a meeting for this Place heard some very good speeches

Sept 28

Sunday and a stormy one to [sic] cleared away at noon wrote three Letters Eas [sic] one to M E S & B A H

PAGE 71

and Mother went out in the afternoon & took a walk

Sept 30

Attended a Ball this Evening saw a good many Pretty Girls

Oct 2

Went to see a sleight of hand Performance this Eving [sic] had a good time

Oct 6

a warm Pleasant day wrote Home to the Friends

Oct 5

went to the PO in the Eving [sic] got a Letter from B A H & two Papers

PAGE 72

Oct 12

Have been Husking corn all the week been in my Plantation to day all right expect go to Winona this [week] to Pre Empt think of leaving this place before long wrote one Letter to day to M E T

Oct 13

Went to the P Office and got three Letters one from Mother one from B A H & one from M E T

PAGE 73

Oct 14

Election day in this place saw quite a good many people in Town wrote three letters one to
Mother one to [B A H] one to M E T

Oct 15

left at 7 oclock for Winona stopped over Night at Utica 30 miles from here saw there the Prettiest Girl I have seen since I have been in the Territory

PAGE 74

Oct 16

left early in the morning for Winona arrived there at 3 oclock safe & sound saw J D Rogers there was glad to see him again

Oct 17

Went to the Land Office early & got my Business done in good season [tad] my face taken to send East saw a good many Indians

PAGE 75

there dressed out very fantastical left at 11 for home reached Utica at 9 in the Evening

Oct 18

left Utica & reached Home at 3 in the afternoon went to the

P Office got a letter from M A Sharp Chicago

Oct 19

wrote only one letter to day in the answer to the one I got Saturday Read in the afternoon & passed the day very

PAGE 76

and passed the day very Pleasantly

Oct 20

Have sold my [Land] to day & took a Note Payable on demand at 3 per cent a Month

Oct 21

A wet Stormy day passed the day in loafing about

Oct 22

Ditto

Oct 23

Ditto

Oct 24

Ditto

PAGE 77

Oct 25

the same as the fore part of the week

Oct 26

wrote home weather cool & cloudy with prospect of rain

Oct 27

clear and cold as the devil

Oct 28

weather cold as yesterday

Oct 29

Have been at work once more to day for the P M clear and cold as ever

PAGE 78

Oct 29

weather cold for the time of year

Oct 30

went into the P Office in the Evening expecting to get a letter but was disappointed

Oct 31

very pleasant for the time of year

Nov 1

warm & pleasant

N 2

wrote three letters home passed the ballance [sic] of the day in reading

PAGE 79

Nov 3

a cold day wind blowing like furry [sic] it is a great country here for high winds went to the P O in the Evening got three Letters from the East one from B A H and two M E T was very much pleased to hear from home again begin to think of leaving the Territory soon for a warmer climate think I will leave in a few weeks

PAGE 80

cloudy and very cold had a slight fall of Snow last Evening

wish I was down the River a ways in the Evening attended a meeting a kind of Prot[estant] one we are having a sort of revival here think there is need enough of one for I was never in a place where there is so much swearing as there is here

PAGE 81

to day is the Presidential Election wish I was where I could vote for Fremont and Freedom[3]

Nov 5

weather clear & rather cold worked half a day saw three Native Americans in the afternoon Dressed in true Indian style

Nov 6

weather cloudy & cold saw two Indians

PAGE 82

Nov 7

a cold Windy day a Party of Red Men came in this morning about twelve in all went to the P Office in the Evening got a letter from Mother

Nov 8

---

3   This indicates that Hamilton supported Republican John C. Frémont of California, who opposed the expansion of slavery into any new states.

clear & very cold did not work to day

Nov 9

Sunday again a pleasant day went out to day to see some Bridgeport Friends had a good visit

PAGE 83

wrote home two letters

Nov 10

Cloudy & cold have done no work to day

Nov 11

Went to the P Office this morning got a letter from M E T clear & cold

Nov 12

wrote one letter home to day M E T very pleasant for the time of year got my Pay for my Land to day

Nov 13

Have been at work to day think I shall

PAGE 84

Stop here awhile longer shall as long as I get the wages I do now [175] per day

Nov 14

Still at work very pleasant weather

Nov 15

worked half a day to day got a letter this morning from M E T

Nov 16

Sunday and a cold day set in the House all day wrote two letters East B A H M E T

PAGE 85

Nov 17

Cloudy & Cold begin to think of leaving soon worked half a day went to the P Office in the Evening but was disappointed

Nov 18

Clear & Pleasan [sic] worked half a day

Nov 19

worked all day weather clear & Pleasant

Nov 20

Thanksgiving day have worked all day to day got a letter last Night from Home

PAGE 86

Nov 21

A damp foggy day worked half a day rained in the afternoon

Nov 22

Weather cool & cloudy worked all day

Nov 23

a stormy morning a regular north East snow storm the first of the season

Nov 24

Worked all day weather mild for the season

Nov 25

Commenced snowing

PAGE 87

again this morning and it looks out of doors like Winter al-though the weather very mild done no work today Received a letter this morning from B A H & wrote one in Return

Nov 26

A cold morning good Sleyging Sleighing worked all day quite Pleasant in the afternoon

Nov 27

Cloudy and rather coll [sic] firstrate [sic] Sleighing

PAGE 88

Worked all day got so that I like the Work Pretty well grow fat on it had venison for Breakfast & dinner to day the first I ever eat very good

Nov 28

A very mild nice day for [Business] worked all day as usual

Nov 29

Clear & very Pleasant a very nice day to work worked all the day Begin to think of leaving soon

PAGE 89

Nov 30

Last day of this month How fast the time gets away it does not seem more than 2 or 3 weeks since I left home Attended Church to day for the first time in a long while heard a good discourse wrote two letters Home in the Evening commence snowing about 4 oclock like f[ ] and bids fair to have a large Snow Storm

PAGE 90

December 1

A mild winter morning good Sleighing worked 1 hour in the forenoon & then quit Begin to look out for a Chance to Ride to Dubuque did not work to day expect to leave this Place to morrow

Dec 2d

A cold windy day Have not worked any to day expected to leave this afternoon for Dubuque but was disappointed a snow storm set in about 4 oclock in the afternoon and

PAGE 91

continued through the Night it was one of the most violent storms of the kind I ever Saw the air was so thick with Snow that a Person could hardly breath [sic] I wish I was in some Place but Minnesota for it is to [sic] cold to suit me

Dec 3d

Last Night was an awful Storm and a cold day Snow Plenty & very deep in Places saw Mr E Fairchild of Bethel to day had quite a

PAGE 92

long talk with him think I will leave in the morning for Dubuque

Dec 4

A very cold morning the thermometer 20 Deg below zero about as cold morning as I ever saw left Rochester at 10 oclock this morning for Dubuque Iowa Rode all day & reached Jordan 22 miles from Rochester & Put up for the Night the road was very bad owing to the depth

PAGE 93

of Snow & we reached to the full exten [sic] that Jordan is a |[hard] road to travel |Bill 75

Dec 5

Left Jordan a [sic] 7 oclock going through Fillmore reached Carmonia⁴ at noon stopped for dinner Left after dinner & Stopped for the Night at Greenfield Passed through[Wan-

---

4   Probably should be Carimona, presently a township in Fill-more Co., MN.

koker]⁵ a small Place 9 miles from Carmania

PAGE 94

Dec 6

Left Greenfield this morning Passed through Burr Oaks
& Elliota⁶ & Crossed over the line into Iowa reached Decorah at 1 o'clock and took dinner found it to be a very Pretty
Place looking a little more like [Civilization] Left Decorah
at 3 oclock & reached Frankville and Stopped for the Night
w Have made a good days Journey to day expect to reach
Dubuque in two days

PAGE 95

more Passed through a Beautiful country to day & one I like
much better than Minnesota

Dec 7 |Send

Left Frankville this morning Passed through Hardin &
Stopped for dinner at Monona reached Garnavillo & stopped
for the Night am now 45 miles from Dubuque h[oping to]
get there to [morrow] Passed through a [   ] [cou]ntry to
re[ach] [   ]⁷

---

5   It appears that neither this Greenfield nor Wankoker places
survived very long.

6   Elliota was and is in Minnesota, and Burr Oak in Iowa.

7   The bottom corner of the page is folded over and too fragile
to unfold.

PAGE 96

Dec 8

Left Garnivillo this morning crossed Turkey River & eat dinner by the way and Put up for the night 14 miles from Dubuque have Passed through a very rough Country to day

Dec 9/Guesd??

Left this morning the 14 mile House and at eleven oclock find myself in Dubuque and Pleased to see

PAGE 97

the River once more took dinner & then crossed the River to Dunleith on the Ice Left at 6 o'clock for Rockford reached there at 12 midnight & stopped over Night with Mr Harris who was supprised [sic] to see me at that time of Night

Dec 10

a Wet & unpleasant to day called to see Mr Norman this morning found him all Right

PAGE 98

Dec 11 Thursday

A Stormy & unpleasant day one week from this morning I

was in Rochester Minn Ter how the time flies away amused myself to day by looking around the City of Rockford

Dec 12

A Beautiful day had an invitation to take dinner with Wm Norman accepted had a very nice call went out to [Uncle]

PAGE 100/99 [two page numbers given for a while]

[Dans] in the afternoon and Passed the Night find them all well

Dec 13 |Sat

A cool morning weather cloudy & looks like a storm went to Town in the afternoon and came back in a snow storm

Dec 14 Sund

A Cold Blustering day sat in the House all day & read the Newspapers a rather long day for me But it Passed at last

PAGE 101/100

Dec 15 Monday

A Clear cold day sit in the House all day and Read N[wks] & & etc. Begin to be uneasy & want to hear from Home so that I can dicide [sic] whether I go East or not shall do one or the other next week Monday

Dec 16 Tues

One week to day since I left the Dubuque and came this side the Mississippi how the time flies a Pleasant

PAGE 102/101

Winters day Rode into to Rockford & bought me an Overcoat coat Pants & vest price $30,00 came back [frost] at Night well Pleased with my Purchase

Dec 17 Wed

Sit in the House all day & Read & Read – a cold day begin to think of leaving soon for some Place to Winter

Dec 18 Thurs

Went to Rockford in the Forenoon went to the Post Office rather

PAGE 103/102

expected to get a Letter but was disappointed came back toward Eve & attended a Donation Party had a very good time saw some very Pretty Girls

Dec 19 Friday

A stormy morning rained all Night last Night but there is

Plenty of Snow left yet it has rained all day like shot sit in the House all day & worked at the old Trade [viz] Brading [sic]

PAGE 104/103

Dec 20 Sat

A cold day Thermometer Six Deg below Zero walked into Town & Passed the day staid Went to the Post Office expecting to get a Letter but Him no come staid [sic] all Night at Mr Harris

Dec 21 Sunday

A mild Winter Day visited the Post Office at noon but did not get any Letter as usual hope the Danbury folks wont [sic]

PAGE 105/104

Condesend [sic] to write me a gain for I dont [sic] want to hear from that Place again I think I will give up Writing Letters to any and either Friend of [sic] Foe for it dont [sic] amount to much at least such is my opinion at Present I almost wish to day I was up in Minnesota again & Passed the Afternoon in the House by the Stove

PAGE 105

meditating upon Mankind in General but more Particular Womankind Oh Woman

Dec 22 Mond

A Cold Cold Morning Thermometer Six Deg below Zero I find the weather so far almost as cold as that of Minnesota went to the Post Office in the afternoon Received three Letters from [Home/the] East urging me to come East immediately expect

PAGE 106

to leave this Evening at eleven o'clock want to be in Danbury Wednesday Evening if Possible to attend G P Smiths Wedding

Dec 23 Tuesday

Another cold morning Thermometer six Deg below Zero did not leave last Evening as I expected as there was no Train to leave Freeport till to day at eleven o'clock was very much disappointed but it can

PAGE 107

not be helped if Nothing happens more than I am aware of I shall leave here to day for Chicago Left Rockford at one o'clock to day and reached Chicago at five this Evening Called on M H T found him & Family well took Tea & stopped for the Night

Dec 24 | Wed

A Pleasant day called on Mr

PAGE 108

Keeler & W K Putnam found them all well Chicago is as lively as ever expect to leave this afternoon at 3,30 for the East Left Chicago & reached Detroit at five this morning Left there at half past five for Winsor crossed the St Clair river and found myself in Canada tis Christmas day my old Friend G P S has I suppose

PAGE 109

Ere this left the Single state of Blessedness for that of Connubial felicity will success attend him & his I should have liked to have been there to seen the Not [sic] tied but it could not be [did] Perhaps it will be Just as well in the End I hope now to be able to reach Home on Friday Evening I expect

PAGE 110

to see this afternoon a sight worth seeing viz Niagra [sic] Falls arrived at the Falls at 3,20 & beheld for the first time in my life the Suspension Bridge & Niagra [sic] falls a Sight worth Seeing left there at 4 o'clock ride all Night and found myself in Albany the next morning left there at 9 & reached NY at 11 o'clock called to see Mr

PAGE 111

Gray & stayed to Dinner left there at 3 ½ oclock for Danbury

arrived safe & sound in Bean
Town at 7 o'clock & stayed all Night at [Guys]

Dec 27

arose & eat breakfast & went down town to see the Natives
& I rather think I saw them all stayed all day and went to
Pembroke at Night

PAGE 112

and found the People all well as usual and myself Home
again but I begin to be sorry that I have come East, but will
try & make the best of it as I am now Home again I will close
this Jour[nal]

PAGE 113

Expenses 1857

[T   z]

Jan   1

cigar 00	03
Salts	04
Pr Stockings	12
Postage Letters	09
1 Hat 1	50
1 [Pin]	06
1 D Paper	04

1 cigar		03
8	[Gristmeal]	12 ½
9	[Subs Tinns smooth]	37 ½
9	two cigars	04
9	1 Paper	05

3 30 12 00
       7   6
23 10   15
33 00
[two illegible lines]

PAGE 114

Memoranda
We[ ]tring Paper & Envelopes
Steel Pens & ink

[several pages torn out] [119 - blank]

PAGE 120

Dec 4 Dinner Buck [Ave] Hotel 30
21   Staid [sic] all Night
at Jordan]H]M   75
Dinner Carminia   25
5   Staid all Night
at Greenfield   1 00

Iowa

Dinner at Decirah 70   25

6   Staid all Night at Frankville   75
         Dinner at Monina   25
7   Staid all Night at Garnivillo   1 00

8   Dinner [Sinoku]
         Staid all Night   25
         at 14 Mile House   75
         Fare M[rgh]   5 00
         $ 10 60

[   ] Extras   1 00

  PAGE 121

A Short Letter
Third Epistle John 13 + 14 verses

Clinton Wheaton Union Mills Laporte County Md

C B Lines
New Haven
Ct

Kansas &c &c
Fowler & Wells
308 [B] [A[nay

PAGE 122

Letters written Commencing May 10 18/56

May   From Chicago
10   G P Smith   1
10   Mother   1
10   M E T1
12   Bro Clark   1
"   M E T2
17   M E T3
17   G P Smith
17   Eli Hamilton
28   M E T4
28   Bro Clark   2
30   M E T5
June
1   B A H1
5   B A H2
7   G P Smith   2

PAGE 123

June
7   M E T6
8   Bro Clark

Rockford Ill
11   G N H
11   M E T7
15   Winona Minnesota
15   Eli Hamilton

15   M E T8
Rochester Minn
19   G N H
19   M E T9
19   M H I | Chicago
19   G H Norris | Ottawa
22   Mother   2
22   G P Smith   3
22   M E T10
22   A Barnum | Dement

PAGE 124

June

29   M E T11
29   B A H3

July

7   A Stevens | La Crosse
10   B A H4
10   M H I | Chicago
10   M E T12
17   G H Norris | Ottawa
17   C A Ironbridge
17   M E T13
17   Mother   3
22   G P Smith   4
24   Bro Clark
24   M E T14

30   B A H5
30   M E T15

Aug

2   M E T16
2   N Hamilton

PAGE 125

Aug

10   Bro Clark   4

Sept

10   B A H21   6   Mother
 10   M E T17   28   9   Brt H
17   M E T18   28   M E T 25
17   G N H   28   Mother

Oct

24   M E T 19   5   10   B A H Sept
2   M E T 20   5   M E T 26
5   Mother 4   12   M E T 27
6   B A H14   7   M E T 28
7   M E T 21   14   19   B A H
7   G P Smith 5   14   Mother
14   M E T 22 Winona 19   M E T 29
16   G P Y 6+   19   M H I [ ]

16   M E T 23   26   M E T 30

Nov

17   G W H   26   12   B A H

Nov

21   B A H8   2   B A H
21   M E T 24   2   Mother   8 [126 – page is much scribbled on, probably by a child]
Nov 2 M E T32
9   M E T33
9   Mother   9 +
12   M E T34
16   M E T35
16   B A H13
20   Bro Clarke   [54]
20   M E T36
25   B A H14
30   B A H15
30   M E T37
Dec   Dunleith Ill
9   M E T
9   B A H16+ 38 +
Rockford Ill
12   G H Norris Ottawa
[inside back cover – much scribbled upon, probably by a child] BA in Rockford
June 13 1856

M T T[   ]
G. N. Hamilton
[N M]
Danbury
[   ]
Fairfield County

Connecticut
18[06]

[some scribbled numbers, sums omitted]

ACKNOWLEDGMENTS

I am extremely grateful for special hospitality and assistance provided to me by the Genealogy Section of the Connecticut State Library in Hartford, which has also so graciously served as custodian of the Hamilton family papers. I am particularly thankful for the assistance of Diane Hassan of the Danbury Museum and Historical Society for her research assistance digging up lost anecdotes of history and providing direction. I wish to thank Kristen N. Keegan for her outstanding research assistance, transliteration and interpretation of the rather unkempt diary of George Norris Hamilton traveling out West. Jane Cormuss has provided superb diligence editing the text. Finally, I would like to express my profound appreciation to Edward R. Hamilton, William A. Hamilton, and Richard Hamilton for their assistance digging up and puzzling out many of the illustrations included herewith. What began as a venture of curiosity evolved into almost five years of walking the burdened, yet historic paths of ancestors. It was a tedious journey, but one not devoid of some rather strange discovery.

PHOTO CREDITS

38	BARK VOLTIGEUR	January 1982 Sketch by Francis H. Schell (1834-1909). From the New York Public Library, no known US copyright restrictions.
66	PLAQUE AT ANTIETAM	Photo by George Glass 2013
70	PLAQUE AT ANTIETAM	Photo by George Glass 2013
71	BURNSIDE'S BRIDGE	Photo by George Glass 2013
80	GEORGE NORRIS HAMILTON/ ELI CLARK HAMILTON	From private collection of Edward R. Hamilton
82	BATTERY B IMAGE	From envelope fragment in *Hamilton-Knapp Collection 1742-1924*, (Hartford: Connecticut State Library, Archive RG 69:7)
86	ELI CLARK HAMILTON/ MARY F. PLOW	From private collection of Edward R. Hamilton
89	ELI CLARK HAMILTON	From private collection of Edward R. Hamilton
96	STARR HAMILTON	From private collection of Edward R. Hamilton
99	PEMBROKE MAP	Courtesy of the Danbury Museum & Historical Society Authority
101	HAMILTON PRESS IMAGE	Image from receipt dated 10 April 1895 in *Hamilton-Knapp Collection 1742-1924*, (Hartford: Connecticut State Library, Archive RG 69:7)
103	EDGAR EDWARD HAMILTON	From private collection of Edward R. Hamilton

104	HAMILTON PRINT SHOP 1904	From Leary, Edward A., John H. Hinton, and Albert E. Hamilton. *60 Years in Danbury 1878–1938.* (The Hamilton Press: Danbury, 1938) p. 10. Photo believed from collection of Ruth H. Mallory, of the Mallory Hat Company.
105	EDGAR HAMILTON SWORD HANDLE	From private collection of author
106	MINNIE ETTA STARR	From private collection of Edward R. Hamilton
111	GEORGE EDGAR HAMILTON	George Washington Patterson, IV, editor, Yale College, *History of the Class of Nineteen Hundred and Fourteen*, Volume One (New Haven: Yale University Press 1914),185. Not in copyright.
112	ALBERT EDWARD HAMILTON	From private collection of Edward R. Hamilton
115	GEORGE NEWTON HAMILTON	From private collection of author
119	HAMILTON DRIVE SIGN	© 2013 George A. Glass
193	GEORGE A. GLASS	© 2014 Nicole Glass

BACK JACKET

VIEW OF DANBURY, CONN. 1875	Library of Congress, Geography and Maps Division. Not in copyright.

BACK FLAP

GEORGE A. GLASS	© 2014 Nicole Glass

BIBLIOGRAPHY

300th Anniversary, The First Congregational Church, 1696–1996. Danbury, Connecticut, May 19, 1996.

Adjutant General's Office. *General Orders Affecting the Volunteer Force 1862.* Washington: Government Printing Office, 1863.

Arnold, Samuel Greene. *History of the State of Rhode Island and Providence Plantations Vol. II. 1701–1790.* Providence, R.I.: Preston & Rounds, 1894.

Bailey, James Montgomery. *History of Danbury, Conn. 1684–1896.* New York: Burr Printing House, 1896.

Clemens, William M. *The Hamilton Family in America.* New York: William M. Clemens, 1913.

Commemorative Biographical Record of Fairfield County, Connecticut, Part II. Chicago: J.H. Beers & Co., 1899.

Commemorative Biographical Record of the Counties of Huron and Lorain, Ohio. Chicago: J.H Beers & Co., 1894.

Croffut, W. A., and John M. Morris. *The Military and Civil History of Connecticut During the War of 1861–65.* New

York: Ledyard Bill, 1868.

Dobson, David, *Scots in New England 1623–1875*. Baltimore, Md.: Genealogical Publishing Co., 2002.

Drake, Samuel G., editor, *New England Historical & Genealogical Register for the year 1851, Vol. V*. Boston: Samuel G. Drake, 1851.

Drury, David. "Connecticut in the French and Indian War." Undated. <http://www.connecticuthistory.org>. Accessed September 18, 2015.

Hamilton, Wayne. *The Hamilton Inheritance* . Snohomish County, Washington: Wayne Hamilton, 2001.

Hamilton–Knapp Collection 1742–1924. Hartford: Connecticut State Library, Archive RG 69:7.

Hoadly, Charles J., editor. *Public Records of the Colony of Connecticut, from May, 1754, to February, 1757, Inclusive.* Hartford: Press of the Case, Lockwood & Brainard Co., 1881.

Hurd, D. Hamilton, editor, *History of Fairfield County, Connecticut*. Philadelphia: J.W. Lewis & Co., 1881.

Jenkins, Robert E. *Jenkins Family Book Being a Partial Record of the Descendants of David Jenkins*. Chicago: Chicago Bar, 1904.

Leary, Edward A., John H. Hinton, and Albert E. Hamilton. *60 Years in Danbury 1878–1938*. Danbury: The Hamilton Press, 1938.

Munger, J.B. *The Munger Book Something of the Mungers 1639–1914*. New Haven: Tuttle, Morehouse & Taylor Company, 1915.

Rensselaer Wickham, Gertrude Van, editor. *Memorial to the Pioneer Women of the Western Reserve (Part 5)*. Cleveland: The Women's Department of the Cleveland Centennial Commission, 1896.

Schildt, John W. *Connecticut at Antietam*. Chewsville, Md: Antietam Publications, 1988.

Starr, Burgis Pratt. *A History of the Starr Family*. Hartford, CT: Case, Lockwood & Brainard Company, 1879.

Warren, Lt. Colonel Charles. "History of the Eleventh Connecticut Volunteer Infantry Regiment." Undated. <www.11thcvi.org/files/11th_history.pdf>. Accessed September 18, 2015.

Wende, Bugler Richard. *Campaign of Light Battery "B," 5th U.S. Artillery*. Phillipsburg, NJ: E. R. Galligan, 1895.

ABOUT THE AUTHOR

George A. Glass grew up in New Jersey. He studied international affairs in Boston, Bologna, Washington, Berlin, and Pittsburgh. From 1977 until 1981 he worked as a lecturer and author in Germany and France. In early 1981 he joined the U.S. Department of State as a career diplomat. He spent 31 years in diplomatic missions, which included Berlin, Moscow, Washington, Tokyo, Bern, Vienna, and Munich. He reached the senior ranks of the Foreign Service winning numerous awards. He is the author of *Cold War Diplomat, Inside U.S. Diplomacy 1981–2011*.

Mr. Glass left the Foreign Service in late 2011. He and his wife divide their time between Garmisch-Partenkirchen, Germany, and a variety of locations in the United States, where their children reside.

www.ingramcontent.com/pod-product-compliance
Lightning Source LLC
Chambersburg PA
CBHW040749150426
42811CB00074B/1958/J